The Creative Cook

Campbell Soup Company

Table of Contents

Introduction

Cooking is a very personal art. It reflects attitudes and creativity as well as knowledge and skill. In earlier times, cooks were restricted by local harvests and climates, yet the history of cooking is a testament to human ingenuity and adaptation to dynamic changes.

In America, we have a great abundance and variety in available foods, but unique time priorities. We tend, in food, as in other things, to want the best quality in the least amount of time.

Using condensed soup as a cooking ingredient helps ease the inexorable pressure of never having enough time. This bright and creative idea was introduced in a Campbell Soup publication in 1916. Since then, many recipes based on that preparation technique have been made available. The Tomato Spice Cake, Green Bean Bake and other suggestions presented in the Campbell Classics Chapter of this book are typical of the quick to prepare and delicious ways of including condensed soup as an ingredient in cooking.

The current American cooking scene, however, is marked by increasingly sophisticated tastes and adventuresome expectations. Our attitudes toward foods and cooking are changing with our lifestyles.

The cookbook reflects these changes. More than 250 recipes have been developed to help prepare all kinds of foods with maximum appeal and imagination and minimum effort. The types of categories selected and the ingredients, techniques and equipment used mirror what seems to have popular appeal in today's world.

In these nine chapters, there are recipes to use on any number of different occasions. They present fascinating challenges and great satisfaction. Here, too, the benefits of cooking with condensed soup has universal application: it makes preparation of time-consuming and sometimes difficult kinds of dishes such as sauces and batters much easier; provides flavor; can be relied upon for consistency. Most important, by eliminating drudgery, condensed soup opens a treasury of creative ideas.

Some of these recipes are adapted from centuries-old traditional dishes. Others have an aura of elegance once produced by a retinue of kitchen assistants. Each has some special flavor, texture, flair. From among all of the recipes offered here we hope many will become your favorites.

Splendid Appetizers and Distinctive Sandwiches

Splendid Appetizers and Distinctive Sandwiches

Food is a hallmark of hospitality. At holiday time, fruited cakes, cookies and sweets are common. In earlier days, travelers gathered at inns renowned for a specific cheese, bread or hot soup. In our own era of informal hospitality, it is a good idea to be like the innkeepers of old and have recipes and ingredients for light, easy to eat but decidedly superior foods.

These hospitality foods come in an array of shapes, sizes, textures and traditions. Sandwiches, crepes, fondues, dips, cheeses are all included in this repertoire. A great many are as appropriate for impromptu hospitality as for appetizers before dinner.

The concept of a before-dinner appetizer has interested man for centuries. The Mandarins of ancient China took pride in offering a great variety. Athenians enjoyed dolmas as early as 350 B.C. and the Romans even had a name for their "tasters," gustotio.

This 10th century description of a Persian hors d'oeuvre tray shows that little has changed in the span of time:

"Here capers grace a sauce vermilion
Whole fragrant odors to the soul are blown....
Here pungent garlic meets the eager sight
And whets with savor sharp the appetite,
While olives turn to shadowed night the day,
And salted fish in slices rims the tray...."

Every country has its traditional appetizers. For the French, it is the hors d'oeuvre, meaning outside the meal. The Italians have their antipasto, the Spanish their tapas or "teasers" which are often shellfish. The Scandanavians are famous for the smorgasbord and the Russians the zakuski.

Many of these creations were time-consuming and complicated to prepare, but today condensed soups provide an easy base for many imaginative offerings.

Notice the Miniature Quiches in the preceding photograph. To prepare them, crepes are folded in a unique way to hold a delicious combination of spinach, cheese and ham in a sauce of cream of mushroom soup. Velvety-smooth Cheese Fondue with Beer is the perfect example of condensed soups' time-saving style. Make this delicious dish starting with condensed Cheddar cheese soup.

While you are looking at the photo, notice the Chicken Stack in the foreground. In it, condensed cream of asparagus soup is used in two ways. First, it sauces the chopped chicken salad spread between the layers of bread and second, it adds flavor and substance to the cream cheese frosting. This elegant creation is a far cry from the first known sandwich.

The Earl of Sandwich, John Montague, was the originator of the sandwich but he probably had no idea that his invention would become so versatile or popular. He created the sandwich purely out of necessity when he was occupied at the gaming tables. He did not want to be interrupted, so he requested that meat be brought to him between two pieces of bread.

Regardless of the history of the sandwich and other recipes in this chapter, these are foods especially adaptable to today's social climate. Even a small selection can be a display of grace and elegance. They demand only a reasonable time for preparation, yet clearly indicate a warm welcome.

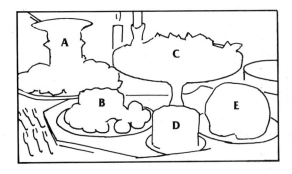

A CHEESE FONDUE WITH BEER
B CHICKEN HORS D'OEUVRES
C MINIATURE QUICHES
D CHICKEN STACKS
E COUNTRY CHEESE BALL

HOT ONION DIP

The condensed soup in this recipe lends its onion flavor to the cheese. Hot peppers add zip!

1 can (10 1/2 ounces) condensed cream of onion soup
1 package (8 ounces) cream cheese, softened

2 tablespoons chili sauce
1 tablespoon chopped hot cherry peppers

With electric mixer or rotary beater, gradually blend soup into cream cheese. Beat just until smooth (overbeating makes dip thin). Stir in chili sauce and peppers; chill. Serve with crackers or chips. Makes about 2 cups.

COUNTRY CHEESE BALL

A small clove of pungent garlic makes its presence known in this cheese ball. After chilling, and rolling the ball in parsley, serve it with assorted crackers.

1 can (11 1/2 ounces) condensed bean with bacon soup
3 cups shredded sharp Cheddar cheese

1/2 cup crumbled blue cheese
Dash cayenne pepper
1 small clove garlic, minced
Chopped parsley or watercress

At low speed of electric mixer, beat soup, cheeses, pepper, and garlic until smooth; chill. Shape into ball; roll in parsley. Serve with crackers. Makes about 3 cups.

COCKTAIL MEATBALLS

A chafing dish is the ideal way to keep these meatballs hot at a party. Provide plates, forks and napkins for the guests.

1 pound ground beef
1/2 pound pork sausage
1/3 cup fine dry bread crumbs
1 egg, slightly beaten
1/3 cup chopped onion
1/3 cup chopped green pepper
1 medium clove garlic, minced

1/8 teaspoon crushed red pepper
2 tablespoons butter or margarine
1 can (10 3/4 ounces) condensed golden mushroom soup
1/4 cup water
1 teaspoon Worcestershire

In bowl, combine beef, sausage, bread crumbs, and egg. Shape into 50 small meatballs (1/2 inch). Broil about 4 inches from heat 3 minutes; turn. Broil 3 minutes more or until done. Meanwhile, in large heavy pan, cook onion and green pepper with garlic and red pepper in butter until tender. Stir in remaining ingredients; add meatballs; simmer 10 minutes. Makes about 5 cups.

MINIATURE QUICHES

Lightly browned crepes are folded to fit into muffin pans. These miniature cups make perfect containers for this excellent quiche filling.

1 can (10 3/4 ounces) condensed cream of mushroom soup
1 package (8 ounces) cream cheese, softened
4 eggs, slightly beaten
1 cup finely chopped fresh spinach

2/3 cup shredded Swiss cheese
1/2 cup finely chopped ham
1/4 cup finely chopped green onions
1/2 teaspoon hot pepper sauce
24 crepes (6-inch diameter)

To make filling: In bowl, blend soup into cream cheese until smooth; stir in remaining ingredients except crepes.

To make appetizers: Lightly oil 24 muffin cups (2 1/2 x 1 1/4"). For each appetizer, place browned side of crepe on flat surface; fold edges toward center to form a square about 3 1/2 inches. Gently press folded crepe into muffin cup, lining bottom and sides (corners of folded crepe will extend above muffin cup). Spoon about 3 tablespoons filling mixture into crepe-lined cups. Bake at 375°F. for 10 minutes. Lay foil over top. Bake 20 minutes more or until done. Remove from muffin cups by gently running spatula around outside of crepes; cool slightly before serving. Makes 24 appetizers.

MEXICALI DIP

A tip of the sombrero to the hostess who serves this fiery hot dip with corn chips.

1 can (11 1/2 ounces) condensed bean with bacon soup
2 cups shredded Monterey Jack cheese*

1/2 cup chopped canned tomatoes
1 tablespoon finely chopped onion
1 tablespoon finely chopped Jalapeño peppers

In saucepan, combine ingredients. Heat until cheese melts; stir often. Serve as a dip with potato or corn chips. Makes about 2 1/2 cups.

*Substitute Monterey Jack cheese with Jalapeño peppers; omit Jalepeño peppers.

BEEFY BLOODY MARY

For an interesting variation to the traditional Bloody Mary try this "beefed-up" version.

1 can (24 fl. oz.) tomato juice
1 can (10 1/2 ounces) condensed beef broth
1 cup vodka

2 tablespoons lemon juice
1/8 teaspoon hot pepper sauce
2 teaspoons Worcestershire

In pitcher, combine ingredients. Serve over cracked ice; garnish with lemon slices. Makes about 5 cups.

CHICKEN EGG ROLLS

If egg roll wrappers are not available in your town, crepes are a fine substitute to hold this chicken-bean sprout filling. Serve with sauce of your choice.

2 cups chopped cabbage
1/4 cup chopped celery
1/4 cup chopped green onions
2 tablespoons salad oil
1 can (5 ounces) chunk
  white chicken
1/4 cup coarsely chopped
  bean sprouts

1/4 cup chopped radishes
1/4 cup chopped water chestnuts
1 tablespoon soy sauce
10 egg roll wrappers or crepes
  (8-inch)
1 egg, slightly beaten
Salad oil

To make filling, in skillet, cook cabbage, celery, and onions in oil until just tender. Add chicken, bean sprouts, radishes, water chestnuts, and soy sauce. To make egg rolls, place 1/4 cup filling just below center of each egg roll wrapper. Roll up, folding in edges to enclose filling; seal seam edge with egg. Chill. Half-fill wok or large saucepan with oil; preheat to 375°F. Fry egg rolls, a few at a time, in hot oil until lightly browned. Drain; keep warm. Serve with sauces. Makes 10 egg rolls.

SWEET AND SOUR SAUCE

Sweet and Sour Sauce is the age old complement to egg rolls.

1/2 can (10 3/4-ounce size)
  condensed chicken broth
1/2 cup brown sugar
1/4 cup red wine vinegar
1 tablespoon soy sauce
1 tablespoon cornstarch
1/4 teaspoon garlic powder
1/8 teaspoon ground ginger

In saucepan, combine ingredients. Cook, stirring until thickened. Makes about 1 cup.

HORSERADISH SAUCE

An oriental-style dip with hot mustard and horseradish goes well with all kinds of egg rolls.

2 tablespoons butter or
  margarine
2 tablespoons flour
1/2 teaspoon dry mustard
1/2 can (10 3/4-ounce size)
  condensed chicken broth
1/2 cup milk
1/4 cup prepared horseradish

In saucepan, melt butter, blend in flour and mustard. Cook a few minutes, stirring constantly. Remove from heat. Add broth and milk, a little at a time, stirring after each addition until smooth. Cook, stirring until thickened. Add horseradish; heat. Makes about 1 1/3 cups.

BLUE CHEESE CROCK

If grandmother's butter crock is in your cupboard, fill it with dip. Or, use a contemporary dip dish and platter.

1 can (10 3/4 ounces) condensed cream of celery soup	1/2 cup crumbled blue cheese
1 package (8 ounces) cream cheese, softened	2 tablespoons finely chopped onion

With electric mixer or rotary beater, gradually blend soup into cream cheese. Beat just until smooth (overbeating makes dip thin). Add remaining ingredients. Chill. Serve as a dip with assorted vegetables. Makes about 2 1/2 cups.

SPINACH CHEESE PUFF

Frozen patty shells, when baked, resemble the Greek pastry, phylo. Roll the shells into 2 layers to sandwich a spinach-feta cheese filling. Bake; cut into squares.

1/2 cup finely chopped onion	5 eggs
2 tablespoons butter or margarine	1/2 pound crumbled feta cheese (1 1/2 cups)
1 pound fresh spinach, cleaned and chopped (about 8 cups)	1/2 teaspoon ground nutmeg
1 can (10 3/4 ounces) condensed creamy chicken mushroom soup	2 packages (10 ounces each) frozen patty shells, thawed
	1 tablespoon cornmeal

In large heavy pan, cook onion in butter until tender. Add spinach; cook until done, stirring. Drain excess liquid. Combine soup, 4 eggs, cheese, and nutmeg; add spinach mixture. Meanwhile, on floured board, arrange 1 package patty shells in two rows. Roll into rectangle (15x10"). Sprinkle cornmeal in bottom of jelly-roll pan (15x10x1"). Line pan with rolled patty shells; spread with spinach mixture. Roll out remaining package patty shells as above; place on spinach mixture. Beat remaining egg; brush on top crust. Bake at 350°F. for 45 minutes or until brown. Cool 25 minutes; cut into squares. Makes 35 squares (2 inch).

HERRING DIP

Slice a variety of colorful vegetables such as carrots . . . on the diagonal . . . to provide a wider dipping surface. A basket might hold unsalted crackers.

1 can (10 3/4 ounces) condensed cream of celery soup	1/2 teaspoon dried dill weed, crushed
1/2 cup sour cream	1 jar (8 ounces) pickled herring tidbits, drained and chopped
1/4 cup finely chopped onion	

In bowl, blend soup, sour cream, onion, and dill; add herring. Chill. Serve with assorted vegetables or crackers. Makes about 2 1/2 cups.

CURRIED CHICKEN PUFFS

Dainty puffs are appealing to adult tastes when the filling is a blend of curry, mushroom soup, chicken and chutney. Water chestnuts add crunch.

Cream Puffs:

1 cup water	1 cup sifted flour
1/2 cup butter or margarine	4 eggs
1/8 teaspoon salt	

Filling:

1/4 cup finely chopped green pepper	1 can (10 3/4 ounces) condensed cream of mushroom soup
1/4 cup finely chopped onion	1 1/2 cups finely chopped cooked chicken
1 medium clove garlic, minced	1/3 cup chopped water chestnuts
1 teaspoon curry powder	2 tablespoons chopped chutney
2 tablespoons butter or margarine	

To make cream puffs: In saucepan, combine water, butter, and salt; bring to boil. Add flour all at once, stirring rapidly until mixture forms ball. Remove from heat; beat in eggs, one at a time, until smooth. Drop by teaspoonfuls on ungreased cookie sheet in 50 small mounds. Bake at 400°F. for 30 minutes or until puffed, brown, and dry; cool.

To make filling: In saucepan, cook green pepper and onion with garlic and curry in butter until tender. Remove from heat; stir in remaining ingredients. Cut tops off cream puffs with sharp knife; fill each with about 1 tablespoon filling. Replace tops. Bake at 400°F. for 10 minutes or until hot. Makes 50 appetizer cream puffs.

FRESH VEGETABLE MARINADE

A vegetable platter of sliced sweet potatoes—a real surprise—zucchini, mushrooms and other favorites draws attention once you explain the Italian marinade.

1 can (10 3/4 ounces) condensed chicken broth	2 cups thinly sliced zucchini
1/4 cup vinegar	1 cup thinly sliced broccoli flowerets
2 tablespoons salad oil	1 cup thinly sliced cauliflowerets
2 tablespoons dry vermouth	1 cup thinly sliced fresh mushrooms
1 package (about 0.9 ounces) mild Italian salad dressing mix	1 cup cherry tomatoes cut in half
2 cups thinly sliced sweet potatoes	

To make marinade, combine broth, vinegar, oil, vermouth, and salad dressing mix. Arrange vegetables in shallow dish; pour marinade over vegetables. Cover. Chill 6 hours or more; stir occasionally. With slotted spoon, arrange vegetables on platter. Makes about 7 cups.

CHEESE FONDUE WITH BEER

Gather round the fondue pot with fondue forks holding bread cubes ready to dip into the rich cheese mixture.

1/2 cup beer
1 large clove garlic, minced
1 pound natural Swiss cheese, cubed or shredded

1 tablespoon flour
1 can (11 ounces) condensed Cheddar cheese soup
Pumpernickel or French bread cubes

In fondue pot or saucepan, simmer beer and garlic. Combine cheese and flour; gradually blend into beer. Heat until cheese melts; stir often. Blend in soup. Heat, stirring until smooth. Spear bread with fork or toothpick and dip into fondue. Makes about 3 cups.

CHICKEN HORS D'OEUVRES

Tarragon lends a very slight taste of licorice to the cheese soup-sour cream sauce served with the hors d'oeuvre.

1 can (11 ounces) condensed Cheddar cheese soup
1 can (5 ounces) chunk white chicken or 1 can (about 7 ounces) tuna, drained and flaked
1 egg, slightly beaten
1/2 cup Italian flavored fine dry bread crumbs

2 tablespoons finely chopped green pepper
2 tablespoons finely chopped green onions
1/4 teaspoon hot pepper sauce
Salad oil
1/4 cup sour cream
Generous dash crushed tarragon leaves

In bowl, mix <u>thoroughly</u> 1/4 cup soup, chicken, egg, bread crumbs, green pepper, green onions, and hot pepper sauce. Shape into 40 small chicken meatballs (1/2 inch). Roll in additional bread crumbs. Half-fill deep fat fryer or large saucepan with oil; preheat to 350°F. Fry meatballs, a few at a time, in hot oil until browned. Drain; keep warm. Meanwhile, in saucepan, combine remaining soup, sour cream, and tarragon. Heat; stir occasionally. Serve with meatballs. Makes 40 appetizers.

FIRESIDE APPLE TODDY

Toddy was once described as a salutary drink meaning its ingredients promoted health.

4 cans (10 1/2 ounces each) condensed beef broth
2 soup cans apple juice
1 soup can water

1/4 cup brandy
1/4 teaspoon ground cinnamon
1/4 teaspoon ground cloves
1/4 teaspoon ground nutmeg

In large saucepan, combine ingredients. Bring to boil; reduce heat. Simmer a few minutes to blend flavors. Serve in mugs; garnish with orange slices. Makes about 9 cups.

STUFFED SHRIMP

It's hard to beat stuffed shrimp as a party appetizer. We make it easy but special by adding bacon, clam chowder and spices to the stuffing mix.

2 slices bacon
1/3 cup finely chopped celery
1/4 cup finely chopped onion
1 large clove garlic, minced
1 teaspoon oregano leaves, crushed
1 can (10 3/4 ounces) condensed Manhattan style clam chowder

1/4 cup chopped parsley
1/8 teaspoon hot pepper sauce
1 cup packaged herb seasoned stuffing mix
1 1/2 pounds medium shrimp (31 to 35/pound)
Lemon juice

To make stuffing, in saucepan, cook bacon until crisp; remove and crumble. Cook celery and onion with garlic and oregano in drippings until tender. Add soup, parsley, bacon, and hot pepper sauce; heat. Stir in stuffing mix. Remove from heat; cover. Let stand 5 minutes. Meanwhile, shell and devein shrimp; do not remove tails. Slit each along vein side almost in two; flatten out. Arrange on broiler pan; brush with lemon juice. Broil 4 inches from heat 5 minutes. Spoon about 1 tablespoon stuffing on each shrimp; brush with lemon juice. Broil 5 minutes more or until done. Makes 45 to 50 appetizers.

WAGON HO FRANKS

Frankfurter pieces, whole mushrooms and green pepper squares mingle in a spicy, hot horseradish sauce.

1 pound frankfurters, cut in half lengthwise
1/4 pound small whole fresh mushrooms (about 1 cup)
1 large green pepper, cut in 1-inch squares
2 tablespoons butter or margarine
1 can (10 1/2 ounces) condensed beef broth

1/3 cup chili sauce
1/4 cup finely chopped onion
2 tablespoons cornstarch
1 tablespoon brown sugar
1 tablespoon prepared horseradish
1 medium clove garlic, minced
1/4 teaspoon hot pepper sauce

Cut frankfurters in 1-inch pieces. In skillet, brown frankfurters and mushrooms and cook green pepper in butter until tender. Stir in remaining ingredients. Cook, stirring until thickened. Makes about 4 cups.

TASCO AVOCADO DIP

Remember to mash the avocado after the dip has chilled. If it goes in too soon the lovely green color may turn brown. Pass corn chips.

1 can (10 3/4 ounces) condensed cream of celery soup
1 package (8 ounces) cream cheese, softened
1 tablespoon finely chopped onion
1 tablespoon chili powder
1 ripe medium avocado

With rotary beater or electric mixer, gradually blend soup into cream cheese. Beat just until smooth (overbeating makes dip thin). Stir in onion and chili powder. Chill. Mash avocado; fold into soup mixture. Serve with corn chips. Makes about 2 cups.

SWEDISH BEEF BURGERS

Scandinavians are noted for their colorful displays of open-face sandwiches. These burgers, with their tomato-sour cream garnish, provide a contrasting sparkle!

1 1/2 pounds ground beef
Salt
Pepper
1 can (10 3/4 ounces) condensed cream of mushroom soup
1/2 cup sour cream
1/8 teaspoon dried dill weed, crushed
6 slices pumpernickel bread, toasted
Tomato slices
Sour Cream

Season beef with salt and pepper; shape into 6 patties. In skillet, brown patties (use shortening if necessary); pour off fat. Stir in soup, sour cream, and dill. Cover; cook over low heat 20 minutes or until done. Stir occasionally. Serve patties on toast; spoon sauce over all. Garnish with tomato and sour cream. Makes 6 open-face sandwiches.

OPEN FACE REUBEN SANDWICH

Here's a Reuben sandwich treated to a saucy combination of onion soup and pickle relish.

1 pound sliced cooked corned beef
8 slices rye bread, toasted
3 cups prepared coleslaw
4 slices (about 4 ounces) Swiss cheese, cut in half
1 can (10 3/4 ounces) condensed cream of onion soup
1/2 cup milk
1/4 cup ketchup
2 tablespoons mayonnaise
2 tablespoons sweet pickle relish
Generous dash hot pepper sauce

On baking sheet, arrange half of corned beef on bread slices; top with coleslaw and remaining corned beef. Cover; bake at 400°F. for 15 minutes or until hot. Top with cheese; bake uncovered until cheese melts. Meanwhile, combine remaining ingredients. Heat; stir occasionally. Serve over sandwiches. Makes 8 open-face sandwiches.

SEASONED CHICKEN TACOS

Garnish with shredded lettuce, cheese or onion. Serve with mugs of iced lemonade.

1 package (3 ounces) cream cheese, softened
1 cup diced cooked chicken
1/2 cup chopped onion
1 tablespoon lemon juice
1/2 teaspoon salt
6 taco shells
Chopped avocado

1 small clove garlic, minced
2 tablespoons salad oil
1 can (10 3/4 ounces) condensed tomato soup
1/4 cup water
Generous dash hot pepper sauce
1 tablespoon chopped Jalapeño peppers

Blend cheese, chicken, 1/4 cup onion, lemon juice, and salt. Fill taco shell; top with avocado. Meanwhile, in saucepan, cook remaining onion with garlic in oil until tender. Add soup, water, hot pepper sauce, and peppers; cook over low heat 15 minutes. Stir occasionally. Serve with tacos. Makes 6 tacos.

WESTERN GROUND BEEF SANDWICH

Fulfill those teens' appetites by serving this western-style beef-chili mixture on toasted, split buns. Pour a cold punch into ice filled glasses.

1 pound ground beef
1 cup chopped onion
1/3 cup diced green pepper
1 can (11 1/4 ounces) condensed chili beef soup
1 can (11 ounces) condensed tomato bisque soup

2 teaspoons Worcestershire
1/4 to 1/2 teaspoon crushed red pepper
1/8 teaspoon ground cumin
Hamburger buns, split and toasted

In saucepan, brown beef and cook onion and green pepper until tender (use shortening if necessary); stir to separate meat. Pour off fat. Add remaining ingredients except buns. Simmer 10 minutes; stir occasionally. Serve on buns. Makes about 4 cups.

TUNA SPREAD A BURGER

A double decker burger. Tuna, eggs and onion are spread on toasted buns and broiled. Then, tomato and cheese slices top each bun for a second broiling.

1 can (10 3/4 ounces) condensed cream of celery soup
1 can (about 7 ounces) tuna, drained and flaked
2 hard-cooked eggs, chopped
2 tablespoons chopped onion

1/4 teaspoon oregano leaves, crushed
4 hamburger buns, split and toasted
8 slices tomato
4 slices (about 4 ounces) Swiss cheese, cut in half diagonally

Mix <u>thoroughly</u> soup, tuna, eggs, onion, and oregano. Spread on buns, covering edges completely. Broil 4 inches from heat 10 minutes or until hot. Top with tomato and cheese; broil until cheese melts. Makes 8 open-face sandwiches.

CHICKEN STACKS

Asparagus soup binds cooked chicken and other ingredients to fill sandwich stacks made with two kinds of bread. A nice addition to your sandwich collection.

1 can (10 3/4 ounces) condensed cream of asparagus soup
2 cups finely chopped cooked chicken
1 cup finely chopped celery
2 tablespoons chopped pimiento
2 teaspoons lime juice
1/8 teaspoon garlic salt
1/8 teaspoon poultry seasoning
12 slices white bread
12 slices pumpernickel bread
11 ounces cream cheese, softened

Reserve 1/3 cup soup. Combine remaining soup, chicken, celery, pimiento, lime juice, and seasonings. To make sandwich stacks, cut 3-inch round from each slice of bread. On 6 rounds of white bread, spread 1/3 chicken mixture; top with 6 rounds of pumpernickel bread. Repeat for 2 more layers ending with pumpernickel bread. To make frosting, beat cream cheese until smooth; gradually blend in reserved soup. Frost top and sides of stacks. Cover; chill until frosting is firm. Garnish if desired. Makes 6 sandwiches.

MEXICAN STEAK SANDWICH

Bean with bacon soup teams with taco sauce, chip steak and pickle relish for a zesty filling for hard rolls. Mexican top-offs are cheese and ripe olives.

1 pound thin wafer-sliced top of the round (chip steak)
4 tablespoons butter or margarine
1/2 cup sliced onion
1 can (11 1/2 ounces) condensed bean with bacon soup
1 can (4 1/2 ounces) prepared taco sauce
2 tablespoons sweet pickle relish
8 long hard rolls, slit and toasted
Chopped fresh tomatoes
Green pepper rings
Shredded process cheese
Shredded lettuce
Sliced ripe olives

In skillet, brown steak in 2 tablespoons butter. Meanwhile, in saucepan, cook onion in remaining butter. Stir in soup; gradually add taco sauce and relish. Heat; stir occasionally. Spread on rolls; top with meat. Garnish with remaining ingredients. Makes 8 sandwiches.

Elegant Soups

Elegant Soups

If bread is the staff of life, soup is the food that restores the spirit. It can be made in wondrous variety. There is truly a soup to fit every nuance of mood, to set perfectly the spirit of the occasion.

Soup goes back to the very earliest roots of man. From its humble beginnings, it has developed as the sign of the aristocrat, the source of inspiration for the artist, a mirror of custom and culture.

From the simple maxim, "Who soups long, lives long," to the worldly-wise "Of soup and love, the first is best," hundreds of sayings have become part of the lore of soup. Brillat-Savarin, the famous 18th century gastronome, even proposed that a woman who could not make soups should not be allowed to marry!

Soups may be classified in three main groups: thin, clear soups like bouillon, broth, and consomme, which may be lightly garnished with vegetables or pasta; cream soups such as bisques or chowders; and thick, hearty ones with various combinations of ingredients including legumes, meat and fish.

Clear soups can be hot or cold, jellied or liquid and may be presented as an elegant overture to a meal. When served in this fashion, they stimulate the appetite and imagination. Selection of the soup is important as it sets the stage for the main production, the entree.

Cream soups can also be served as the appetizer, or may play a more central role in a light supper or luncheon. Again, good planning is important, so the soup functions as the counterpoint of flavor, texture, color and temperature to the rest of the meal.

These versatile soups—both cream and clear—have also traditionally been used as a beverage to be sipped when reading or studying, or after brisk winter walks, or as a mid-morning or afternoon "break." Soup has long been food and drink for the weary spirit.

Heavy, hearty soups are the meal-in-one dishes that have nourished mankind for centuries. These had their roots in the peasant menu but, like home weaving, they have suffered from cyclical winds of fashion. Once people became more affluent, their country dishes were shunned. Today, however, the tide is turning back to thick, satisfying soups as main courses.

Good stock is the foundation of good soup. Traditionally, it has been produced through long, slow cooking of meat, poultry or fish with vegetables for flavoring. Now this time-consuming procedure can be eliminated if you use canned condensed soups as the base for creative soup-making. The recipe for chilled Cucumber A La Creme Soup is quickly put together by starting with condensed chicken broth and blending it with cucumbers, onion and cream.

The preceding photograph illustrates a few of the excellent recipes that can be made with condensed soups.

Preparation time for the Old Fashioned Vegetable Soup is considerably shortened by using condensed beef broth and condensed vegetable soup instead of simmering a stock for many long hours. Time is saved yet the flavor is not compromised.

Sometimes, combining two condensed soups, such as tomato and consomme, produces a base with a consistency in flavor which would be difficult to repeat time after time starting from scratch. For example, these soups, when mixed, make an excellent and quick beginning for Tomato Mushroom Consomme.

Beautiful main course soups like Brunswick Stew, Pot au Feu, Shellfish Chowder, Bouillabaisse, Ukranian Borscht, and others included here, which are usually time consuming to prepare, can readily be considered for today's menus, thanks to condensed soups. This chapter, with recipes from many national cuisines, is an adventure in tastes and flavors.

The history of soup is long and colorful. There is speculation as to just how prehistoric man first boiled foods, and thus made soup. Since pottery did not evolve until about 6000 B.C., soup-makers before that had to rely on nature's provisions for containers. One theory proposes that pits were dug in the ground and lined with overlapping stones to prevent seepage and then filled with liquid to be "cooked." The water was brought to a boil by heating other stones and dropping them into the water.

Another idea suggests that concave mollusk or amphibian shells served as stewing pots. Still another points to the use of animal skins suspended over the fire as cooking utensils.

One fact is certain: people have been writing about soup for a long time. Two early literary references talk about lentil soup. The first is a Biblical reference in Genesis about Esau selling his birthright to his brother Jacob for lentil soup. The other is a recipe for lentil and haricot bean soup from the first known cookbook written by the Roman Apicius in the first century A.D.

During the Middle Ages, soup was an important mainstay of the peasant diet, often feeding large numbers of people in times of war and famine. On the other end of the scale, the aristocracy indulged themselves on soups, sometimes feasting on four or more different varieties during the course of one banquet. Because of the limited number of eating implements at this time, diners ate their soup by soaking bread in it and then eating the bread.

Soup has played an important role in the lives of many famous people, even affecting the course of war, politics and music. When George Washington was dispairing at the fate of his troops during the winter of 1777-1778 at Valley Forge, he called on his chef to create a morally uplifting dish for his suffering troops. The chef produced pepper pot soup from a few scanty provisions, and rallied the troops.

Queen Elizabeth I and Queen Victoria both enjoyed starting their busy days with mutton broth for breakfast. Guiseppe Verdi even claimed that his inspiration for composing music came from a steaming bowl of soup.

To soup goes the credit for the addition of the word, restaurant, to our language. In the mid 1700's in France, soups were called restaurants, the French word for restorative, because they were rumored to have therapeutic powers. A Parisian named Boulanger, in an effort to advertise that he sold soups, hung the name restaurant on a signboard and proclaimed: "Come all ye that labor and I will restore you." Gradually, the word restaurant became identified with an eating place instead of with soup.

Soup was one of man's first convenience foods: travelers on the Mayflower subsisted largely on soups hung in pots from overhead beams. In winter, New Englanders hung pots of soup in outdoor sheds with a paddle in the middle of the pot. Then when the mixture froze, the pot would be removed and the hunk of soup would be hung by a hole in the paddle handle. As needed, chunks were chopped off and heated.

At the end of the 19th century, Abram Anderson and Joseph Campbell introduced canned condensed soup. A few years later, in 1900, The Campbell Soup Company gained international recognition. A gold medallion, signifying excellence, was awarded to Campbell at the Paris Exhibition that year, and the familiar red and white can still proudly bears the medallion.

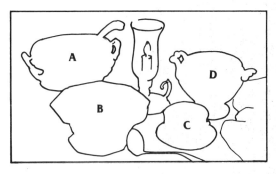

A OLD FASHIONED VEGETABLE SOUP
B CURRIED CAULIFLOWER POTAGE
C TOMATO MUSHROOM CONSOMME
D CREAM OF ASPARAGUS SOUP

CURRIED CAULIFLOWER POTAGE

When cauliflower and cherry tomatoes are at their very best, this is the soup-for-the-season.

1 can (11 ounces) condensed
   Cheddar cheese soup
1/2 cup sour cream
1/2 teaspoon curry powder
1 soup can water

1 cup small cauliflowerets
   parboiled 5 minutes
1/2 cup quartered cherry tomatoes
2 tablespoons sliced green onions

In saucepan, blend soup, sour cream, and curry; gradually stir in water. Heat; stir occasionally. Add remaining ingredients. Chill 6 hours or more. Makes about 4 cups.

TOMATO MUSHROOM CONSOMME

Mushrooms browned in butter, with fresh dill, impart a very special taste to this consomme-tomato soup.

2 cups sliced fresh mushrooms
   (about 1/2 pound)
1/4 cup chopped fresh dill
   weed or 1/2 teaspoon dried
   dill weed, crushed
1 tablespoon butter or
   margarine
1 can (10 1/2 ounces) condensed
   consomme

1 can (10 3/4 ounces) condensed
   tomato soup
1 1/2 soup cans water
1/4 cup diagonally sliced
   green onions
1/4 cup chopped parsley
1 teaspoon lemon juice

In saucepan, brown mushrooms with dill in butter. Add remaining ingredients. Bring to boil; reduce heat. Simmer 5 minutes to blend flavors. Makes about 5 cups.

BLACK BEAN SOUP WITH SHERRY

Some simmering soups like a little sherry. A swirl of sour cream enhances this rich South American soup.

2 cans (11 ounces each)
   condensed black bean soup
1 can (10 1/2 ounces) condensed
   beef broth

1 1/2 soup cans water
1/2 cup sherry

In saucepan, stir black bean soup until smooth; gradually blend in beef broth, water, and sherry. Heat; stir occasionally. Garnish with sour cream or lemon slices. Makes about 5 1/2 cups.

ASPARAGUS LEEK SOUP

It doesn't have to be asparagus season to enjoy a soup of the same name. This golden asparagus soup with a hint of mace is ready in minutes.

1 cup shredded carrot	1/4 cup butter or margarine
1 cup sliced leeks or green onions	3 cans (10 3/4 ounces each) condensed cream of asparagus soup
1/4 teaspoon ground mace	3 soup cans water

In saucepan, cook carrots and leeks with mace in butter until tender. Add remaining ingredients. Heat; stir occasionally. Makes about 7 1/2 cups.

For Chilled Soup: Prepare recipe as above; chill 6 hours or more.

GREEK TUNA SOUP

Greek people consider lemon an important ingredient in soup making. Added to tuna in a chicken with rice soup, it's exciting. You must prepare some soon.

2 cans (10 1/2 ounces each) condensed chicken with rice soup	1 can (about 7 ounces) tuna, drained and flaked
1 1/2 soup cans water	2 eggs
	3 tablespoons lemon juice

In large saucepan, combine soup, water, and tuna. Heat; stir occasionally. Remove from heat. Beat eggs until light and frothy; gradually add lemon juice and 1 cup hot soup. Slowly stir egg mixture into soup. Cook a few minutes over very low heat, stirring until egg is thoroughly blended with soup. Do not boil. Serve immediately (overheating will cause curdling). Garnish with lemon slices. Makes about 6 cups.

CREAM OF ASPARAGUS SOUP

Cucumber, radish and green onion pieces form a kaleidoscope of color against the light green of asparagus soup.

1 can (10 3/4 ounces) condensed cream of asparagus soup	1/2 cup chopped cucumber
1 soup can water	1/4 cup thinly sliced radishes
	2 tablespoons chopped green onions

In saucepan, stir soup; gradually add water. Stir in cucumber, radishes, and green onions. Heat; stir occasionally. Garnish with sour cream. Makes about 2 1/2 cups.

For Chilled Soup: Prepare recipe as above; chill 6 hours or more.

SHELLFISH CHOWDER

Scallops and shrimp combined with Cheddar cheese and celery soup make an aristocratic soup. Serve as a main dish or first course.

2 cups sliced fresh
mushrooms (1/2 pound)
1 cup chopped onion
1 large clove garlic, minced
1/4 teaspoon chervil leaves,
crushed
1/4 cup butter or margarine
2 cans (11 ounces each)
condensed Cheddar cheese soup

1 can (10 3/4 ounces) condensed
cream of celery soup
1 soup can water
1/2 cup chablis or other dry
white wine
1 pound scallops
1 pound medium shrimp
(31 to 35/pound), shelled
and deveined

In large saucepan, brown mushrooms and cook onion with garlic and chervil in butter until tender. Add soups; gradually stir in water and wine. Add scallops and shrimp. Bring to boil; reduce heat. Simmer 10 minutes or until fish is done. Stir occasionally. Makes about 10 cups.

FRESH SPINACH SOUP

Shallots and nutmeg lend the final touch to this elegant cream of spinach soup.

3 cups finely chopped fresh
spinach
1/4 cup thinly sliced
shallots or green onions
2 tablespoons butter or
margarine

2 cans (10 3/4 ounces each)
condensed cream of celery soup
1 1/2 soup cans milk
1/2 soup can water
2 teaspoons lemon juice
1/4 teaspoon ground nutmeg

In saucepan, cook spinach and shallots in butter until tender. Add remaining ingredients. Heat; stir occasionally. Makes about 6 cups.

CHICKEN VEGETABLE SOUP

Make way for that cooked chicken in your refrigerator. By combining two condensed soups, diced chicken and seasonings, there'll be lots of soup for supper.

1/4 cup chopped onion
1/4 teaspoon rosemary
leaves, crushed
2 tablespoons butter or
margarine
1 can (10 3/4 ounces) condensed
cream of celery soup

1 can (10 1/2 ounces) condensed
vegetarian vegetable soup
1 1/2 soup cans water
2 cups diced cooked chicken
1 tablespoon chopped parsley
Dash pepper

In saucepan, cook onion with rosemary in butter until tender. Add remaining ingredients. Heat; stir occasionally. Makes about 6 cups.

CARROT PUREE A LA CRECY

Crecy, a little French town was known for the quality of its carrots. Since the vegetable was so popular, a number of dishes included carrots, among them soup.

1 can (10 3/4 ounces) condensed chicken broth
1 pound medium carrots, sliced (about 3 cups)
1/2 cup chopped onion
1 can (10 3/4 ounces) condensed cream of chicken soup

1/2 cup sour cream
1 soup can milk
1/4 teaspoon salt
1/8 teaspoon ground mace
Generous dash pepper

In saucepan, combine broth, carrots, and onion. Cover; cook over low heat until carrots are very tender. Pour into blender; blend until smooth. In saucepan, combine soup, sour cream, and milk; add carrot mixture and seasonings. Heat; stir occasionally. Serve immediately. Makes about 4 1/2 cups.

For Chilled Soup: Prepare recipe as above; do not add sour cream. Chill 6 hours or more. Before serving, stir in sour cream. Thin to desired consistency with additional milk.

LOTUS SOUP

A lovely light chicken soup with oriental-style cut vegetables. Nice served in lotus bowls.

1 cup diagonally sliced celery
1/2 cup diagonally sliced green onions
1/8 teaspoon ground ginger
3 tablespoons butter or margarine
1 can (10 3/4 ounces) condensed cream of chicken soup

1 can (10 3/4 ounces) condensed chicken broth
1 1/2 soup cans water
1 cup cabbage cut in long thin shreds
1 cup chopped fresh spinach
1 teaspoon soy sauce

In saucepan, cook celery and onion with ginger in butter until tender. Stir in soups and water. Add remaining ingredients. Heat; stir occasionally. Makes about 5 1/2 cups.

YOGURT SOUP

You'll be ecstatic over the flavor of this chicken-yogurt soup spiced with a bit of mace.

1 can (10 3/4 ounces) condensed cream of chicken soup
1 cup plain yogurt

1 tablespoon honey
1/8 teaspoon ground mace
1 soup can milk

In saucepan, blend soup, yogurt, honey, and mace. Stir in milk. Heat; stir occasionally. Garnish with watercress. Makes about 2 1/2 cups.

FISH CHOWDER MARGUERY

Fresh fillets of white fish with pimiento, watercress and laced with wine, make an elegant chowder to serve on special occasions.

1 can (10 3/4 ounces) condensed
   cream of celery soup
1 soup can water
1/4 cup sauterne or other
   dry white wine
1 pound fillet of white fish,
   cut in 2-inch pieces

1/4 cup pimiento strips
1/4 cup chopped watercress
1 teaspoon chervil leaves,
   crushed
1/2 teaspoon garlic salt
Dash pepper

In saucepan, combine ingredients. Bring to boil; reduce heat. Simmer 10 minutes or until done; stir occasionally. Makes about 4 cups.

CHINESE RICE SOUP

Spicy ginger and crisp vegetables give this an oriental touch.

3 cans (10 3/4 ounces each)
   condensed chicken broth
3 soup cans water
2 cups cubed cooked chicken
1 package (10 ounces) frozen
   chopped spinach

1 cup thinly sliced celery
1/4 cup soy sauce
1/2 teaspoon ground ginger
1 cup quick-cooking rice,
   uncooked
1/2 cup sliced radishes

In large saucepan, combine all ingredients except rice and radishes. Bring to boil; add rice and radishes. Reduce heat; simmer 5 minutes or until done. Stir occasionally. Serve with additional soy. Makes about 11 cups.

MEDITERRANEAN FISH SOUP

Many good foods blend together in this fish soup . . . broth, tomatoes, white wine and herbs.

1 can (about 16 ounces)
   tomatoes, cut up
1/2 cup sauterne or other
   dry white wine
1/4 cup chopped parsley
1 teaspoon basil leaves,
   crushed

1 can (10 3/4 ounces) condensed
   chicken broth
1/8 teaspoon sugar
Generous dash pepper
1 pound fillets of white fish,
   cut in 2-inch pieces

In saucepan, simmer tomatoes, wine, parsley, and basil about 2 minutes. Add remaining ingredients. Bring to boil; reduce heat. Simmer 10 minutes or until done. Stir occasionally. Makes about 5 cups.

GARDEN VEGETABLE SOUP

Take a tip from the French who shred lettuce into many excellent dishes. It's a natural flavor-mate for carrots, celery and onion in this soup.

1 cup shredded lettuce
1/2 cup thinly sliced carrot
1/2 cup chopped celery
1/2 cup chopped onion

3 tablespoons butter or margarine
1 can (10 3/4 ounces) condensed
  chicken broth
1 soup can water

In saucepan, cook lettuce, carrot, celery and onion in butter until tender. Add broth and water. Heat; stir occasionally. Makes about 4 cups.

CANDLELIGHT SOUP

Stimulate your appetite for a lovely dinner by candlelight with this delicate flavored puree of pea soup.

1/2 cup finely chopped green
  onions
2 tablespoons butter or
  margarine
1 package (10 ounces) frozen
  peas, cooked and drained

1/2 cup watercress
1 can (10 3/4 ounces) condensed
  chicken broth
1/2 cup light cream
1/4 cup water
1/8 teaspoon ground nutmeg

In saucepan, cook onions in butter until tender. In blender, combine onion, peas, and watercress; blend until smooth. Gradually blend in remaining ingredients; blend until smooth. Pour into saucepan. Heat; stir occasionally. Makes about 3 1/2 cups.

HERBED TOMATO SOUP

A tomato soup redolent of savory and basil. Float a pat of butter in each serving for added richness.

1 can (10 3/4 ounces) condensed
  tomato soup
1 soup can water

1/8 teaspoon ground savory
1/8 teaspoon basil leaves,
  crushed

In saucepan, combine soup, water, savory, and basil. Simmer a few minutes to blend flavors. Top each serving with a pat of butter and chopped parsley. Makes about 2 cups.

MONTEREY SPINACH SOUP

Coral shrimp and deep green spinach leaves stand out in a burst of color as they simmer in rich chicken broth. Serve with sesame seed sticks.

2 cans (10 3/4 ounces each) condensed chicken broth
2 cups fresh spinach torn in bite-size pieces

1 cup cooked shrimp
1 cup sliced fresh mushrooms (about 1/4 pound)
2 teaspoons soy sauce

In saucepan, combine ingredients. Heat; stir occasionally. Makes about 4 1/2 cups.

VEGETABLE CLAM CHOWDER

One need not be a northerner to enjoy clam chowder. This version with zucchini and noodles is a more sophisticated cousin to the rustic chowder of colonial times.

1 cup coarsely chopped zucchini
1/2 cup chopped onion
1 medium clove garlic, minced
1 tablespoon butter or margarine
1 can (10 3/4 ounces) condensed New England clam chowder

1 can (10 1/2 ounces) condensed golden vegetable noodleO's soup
1 1/2 soup cans milk
Generous dash cayenne pepper
2 hard-cooked eggs, sliced

In saucepan, cook zucchini and onion with garlic in butter until tender. Add remaining ingredients. Heat; stir gently now and then. Makes about 6 cups.

TOMATO SOUP SUPREME

A splash of wine—a hint of herbs—and you have an unusual appetizer soup.

1 can (10 3/4 ounces) condensed tomato soup
1 soup can water
2 tablespoons sweet Vermouth

1/8 teaspoon basil leaves, crushed
Generous dash oregano leaves, crushed

In saucepan, combine ingredients. Heat; stir occasionally. Garnish with Parmesan cheese croutons. Makes about 2 1/2 cups.

PASTA AND PEPPER SOUP

The Italian cuisine was the inspiration for this soup with its chick peas and shell macaroni.

1/2 cup chopped green pepper
1 large clove garlic, minced
1/4 teaspoon rosemary leaves, crushed
2 tablespoons olive oil
3 cans (10 3/4 ounces each) condensed tomato soup

3 soup cans water
1 can (about 16 ounces) chick peas or kidney beans, drained
1 cup cooked small shell macaroni
2 teaspoons chopped anchovy fillets
Grated Parmesan cheese

In large saucepan, cook green pepper with garlic and rosemary in oil until tender. Stir in soup and water. Add remaining ingredients except cheese. Heat; stir occasionally. Serve with cheese. Makes about 9 1/2 cups.

BOUILLABAISSE

People who claim they don't like fish will adore this seafood stew after the first spoonful. Ladle it piping hot into warm soup bowls. Serve with sea toast or bread.

1 cup chopped celery
1/2 cup chopped green pepper
1/3 cup chopped onion
1 medium clove garlic, minced
1 large bay leaf
1/2 teaspoon thyme leaves, crushed
1/4 teaspoon crushed red pepper
3 tablespoons butter or margarine

2 cans (11 ounces each) condensed tomato bisque soup
2 soup cans water
2 tablespoons lemon juice
2 tablespoons chopped parsley
1 pound fillets of halibut, cut in 2-inch pieces
1 package (6 ounces) frozen Alaskan King crab meat, thawed and drained
1/2 pound medium raw shrimp (about 16), shelled and deveined

In large saucepan, cook celery, green pepper, and onion with garlic, bay leaf, thyme, and red pepper in butter until tender. Add remaining ingredients. Cook 10 minutes or until done. Stir gently now and then. Remove bay leaf. Makes about 10 cups.

SOUP INDIENNE

Apple and chutney are fine accompaniments to any curried dish. Here they boost flavor in two creamed soups.

2 cans (10 3/4 ounces each) condensed cream of asparagus soup
1 can (10 3/4 ounces) condensed cream of celery soup

1 teaspoon curry powder
2 soup cans water
1 cup chopped apple
1 tablespoon chopped chutney

In saucepan, blend soups and curry powder; gradually stir in water. Add apple and chutney. Heat; stir occasionally. Pour into blender; blend until smooth. Makes about 7 1/2 cups.

BRUSSELS BISQUE

Baby Brussels sprouts enhance the flavor of this creamy chicken-potato bisque.

4 slices bacon
1/4 cup sliced green onions
1 can (10 3/4 ounces) condensed
  cream of chicken soup
1 can (10 3/4 ounces) condensed
  cream of potato soup
1 soup can milk

1/2 soup can water
1 package (10 ounces) frozen
  deluxe baby Brussels sprouts,
  cooked and drained
1/2 cup cut up canned tomatoes
1/4 teaspoon caraway seed

In saucepan, cook bacon until crisp; remove and crumble. Pour off all but 2 table-spoons drippings. Cook onions in drippings until tender. Add remaining ingredients except bacon. Heat; stir occasionally. Garnish with bacon. Makes about 5 1/2 cups.

ORIENTAL SOUP

The Chinese use chicken broth as the base for many soups. With bean sprouts, ginger root and pea pods, this recipe has the flavor of the Orient.

3 cans (10 3/4 ounces each)
  condensed chicken broth
3 soup cans water
1 can (about 16 ounces) bean
  sprouts, drained
3 cups ham cut in thin strips
  (about 1 pound)

1/3 cup teriyaki sauce
4 thin slices ginger root
2 cups diagonally sliced carrots
1 package (6 ounces) frozen
  pea pods
1 1/2 cups fresh spinach torn in
  bite-size pieces

In large heavy pan, combine broth, water, bean sprouts, ham, teriyaki sauce, and ginger. Simmer 10 minutes. Add carrots and pea pods; simmer 5 minutes more or until done. Add spinach. Remove ginger before serving. Serve with additional teriyaki sauce. Makes about 16 cups.

BEEF BROTH PRINTANIER

The French word printanier means a mixture of vegetables. While French chefs may cut the vegetables with a special kitchen utensil, you need only a good sharp knife.

2 cans (10 1/2 ounces each)
  condensed beef broth
2 soup cans water
1/2 cup thin carrot sticks
  (2-inches long)

1/2 cup thin green pepper strips
  (2-inches long)
1/3 cup diagonally sliced
  green onions
1/2 cup sliced cherry tomatoes

In saucepan, combine all ingredients except tomatoes. Bring to boil; reduce heat. Cover; simmer 10 minutes or until done. Stir occasionally; add tomatoes. Makes about 5 1/2 cups.

ITALIAN ESCAROLE SOUP

Escarole can turn into an elegant green when it becomes an integral part of a soup. Here it simmers in chicken broth, wine and herbs.

1/2 cup sauterne or other dry
    white wine
1 teaspoon basil leaves,
    crushed
1 can (about 8 ounces)
    tomatoes, cut up

2 cans (10 3/4 ounces each)
    condensed chicken broth
1 1/2 cups water
4 cups escarole torn in
    bite-size pieces

In saucepan, simmer wine, basil, and tomatoes about 2 minutes. Add remaining ingredients. Cover; cook over low heat 15 minutes or until done. Stir occasionally. Makes about 6 cups.

CHILI BEAN AND BACON SOUP

If Saturday's soup day at your house your children should invite friends. With this southwestern-style soup you can serve crackers, milk and fruit for dessert.

2 slices bacon
1/2 cup chopped celery
1 cup sliced onion
2 tablespoons chopped green
    pepper
1 medium clove garlic, minced
1 teaspoon chili powder

1 can (11 1/2 ounces) condensed
    bean with bacon soup
1 can (11 1/4 ounces) condensed
    green pea soup
1 1/2 soup cans water
1 can (about 16 ounces) tomatoes,
    cut up

In saucepan, cook bacon until crisp; remove and crumble. Cook celery, onion, and green pepper with garlic and chili until tender. Blend in soups; gradually stir in water. Add tomatoes. Heat; stir occasionally. Garnish with bacon. Makes about 6 1/2 cups.

MUSHROOM CARROT CONSOMME

Condensed consomme paves the way for easy—quick "start-the-meal" soup.

1/2 cup sliced fresh mushrooms
1/4 cup thin carrot sticks
    (1-inch long)
1/4 cup chopped celery

1 tablespoon butter or
    margarine
1 can (10 1/2 ounces) condensed
    consomme
1 soup can water

In saucepan, combine ingredients. Heat; stir occasionally. Makes about 3 cups.

SHERRIED CRAB SOUP

Crab in any form is almost a luxury, yet everyone should have the opportunity to savor it. What better way than in a creamy soup spiked ever so lightly with sherry?

1/2 cup chopped onion
1/2 teaspoon dried dill weed, crushed
2 tablespoons butter or margarine
1 can (10 3/4 ounces) condensed cream of celery soup

1 soup can milk
1 cup flaked cooked crab meat
1/4 cup sherry
Generous dash hot pepper sauce

In saucepan, cook onion with dill in butter until tender. Stir in soup, milk, crab, sherry, and hot pepper sauce. Heat; stir occasionally. Makes about 4 cups.

POT AU FEU

Stretch that expensive sirloin steak. Use it in a main course soup. Simmering in beef broth, with vegetables and herbs, you'll see why this soup is a French classic.

1 pound sirloin steak (1-inch thick)
2 cups sliced fresh mushrooms (about 1/2 pound)
1 cup thinly sliced carrots
1/4 cup sliced green onions
1 teaspoon caraway seed
1/8 teaspoon ground cumin seed
1 medium bay leaf

1/8 teaspoon pepper
2 tablespoons salad oil
2 cans (10 1/2 ounces each) condensed beef broth
1 can (12 fl. oz.) "V-8" juice
1 cup beet juice
1 1/2 cups chopped fresh tomatoes (2 medium)

Freeze meat 1 hour to firm (makes slicing easier). Slice into very thin strips. In skillet, brown mushrooms and cook carrots and onions with seasonings in oil until tender; push to one side. Add meat; cook until color just changes. Add remaining ingredients. Heat; stir occasionally. Makes about 8 cups.

SHRIMP GUMBO

Gumbo in minutes? Yes, and in this particular recipe with its canned chicken with rice soup, you have a southern family favorite.

1 can (10 3/4 ounces) condensed chicken gumbo soup
1 can (10 1/2 ounces) condensed chicken with rice soup

1 1/2 soup cans water
2 cups frozen cleaned raw shrimp
1 cup cooked cut green beans
Generous dash cayenne pepper

In saucepan, combine ingredients. Bring to boil; reduce heat. Simmer 5 minutes; stir occasionally. Serve with garlic flavored croutons. Makes about 6 cups.

ZUCCHINI AND CHEDDAR CHEESE SOUP

Zucchini and tomatoes lend brightness to this creamy cheese soup. The subtle flavor of garlic and thyme add distinction.

1 cup sliced zucchini squash
1 small clove garlic, minced
1/4 teaspoon thyme leaves, crushed
2 tablespoons butter or margarine

1 can (11 ounces) condensed Cheddar cheese soup
1 soup can water
1/2 cup drained chopped canned tomatoes

In saucepan, cook zucchini with garlic and thyme in butter until tender. Add soup; gradually stir in water and tomatoes. Heat; stir occasionally. Makes about 3 1/2 cups.

BROCCOLI LETTUCE POTAGE

Two garden greens in a rich cream base make this beautiful to the eye as well as interesting to the taste buds.

1/2 cup sliced green onions
2 tablespoons butter or margarine
1 can (10 3/4 ounces) condensed cream of celery soup

1 soup can milk
1/2 cup cooked chopped broccoli
1/2 cup shredded lettuce
1/8 teaspoon Worcestershire

In saucepan, cook onions in butter until tender; blend in remaining ingredients. Heat; stir occasionally. Makes about 3 cups.

GERMAN BEER SOUP

Cheese and beer are liked by German people. Here they are a plus in green pea soup. To serve with the soup: garlicky pumpernickel and rye bread cubes.

3 cans (11 1/4 ounces each) condensed green pea soup
1 soup can water
1 can (12 fl. oz.) beer
2 cups shredded sharp Cheddar cheese

1/2 cup butter or margarine
1 medium clove garlic, minced
2 cups pumpernickel bread cubes
2 cups rye bread cubes

In large saucepan, stir soup; gradually blend in water and beer. Simmer a few minutes to blend flavors. Add cheese; heat until cheese melts. Stir occasionally. Meanwhile, in skillet, melt butter with garlic; add bread cubes. Cook over low heat, stirring constantly until bread cubes are browned. Serve with soup. Makes about 7 cups.

CURRIED CHICKEN WITH RICE SOUP

The natural sweetness of raisins smooths the hot flavor of curry in this quick-to-make soup.

1/4 cup diagonally sliced
  celery
1/2 teaspoon curry powder
1 tablespoon butter or
  margarine

1 can (10 1/2 ounces) condensed
  chicken with rice soup
1 soup can water
1/4 cup raisins

In saucepan, cook celery with curry powder in butter until tender. Add remaining ingredients. Heat; stir occasionally. Makes about 2 1/2 cups.

SHRIMP VEGETABLE BISQUE

Mushrooms, shallots and asparagus, with a measure of white wine, highlight the flavor of cream of shrimp soup. Serve with cheese crackers and a salad.

1 cup sliced fresh mushrooms
  (about 1/4 pound)
1 tablespoon chopped shallots
  or green onions
Dash crushed tarragon leaves
2 tablespoons butter or
  margarine

1 can (10 3/4 ounces) condensed
  cream of shrimp soup
1 soup can milk
1 cup cooked cut asparagus
1/4 cup chablis or other dry
  white wine

In saucepan, brown mushrooms and cook shallots with tarragon in butter until tender. Add remaining ingredients. Heat; stir occasionally. Makes about 3 1/2 cups.

BRUNSWICK STEW

A variation of an old American stew. This hearty, stick-to-the-ribs dish was a favorite in colonial times.

2 cans (10 3/4 ounces each)
  condensed chicken broth
2 cups diced cooked pork
1 can (about 16 ounces)
  tomatoes, cut up
1 cup ketchup
1/2 cup finely chopped onion
1/2 medium lemon, thinly sliced

2 tablespoons vinegar
1 tablespoon Worcestershire
1/2 teaspoon crushed red pepper
1 can (about 8 ounces) whole kernel
  golden corn, drained
1 can (about 8 ounces) lima beans,
  drained

In large heavy pan, combine all ingredients except corn and lima beans. Bring to boil; reduce heat. Simmer 30 minutes; stir occasionally. Add corn and lima beans; heat. Remove lemon slices. Makes about 7 cups.

LEBANESE LAMB SOUP

Lamb is the meat of mid-eastern countries. Teamed with eggplant and garlic, then combined with tomato bisque soup, the result is a simmering saucepan of wholesome goodness.

1 pound well-trimmed lamb,
  cut in 1/2-inch cubes
1/2 cup sliced fresh mushrooms
2 cups cubed eggplant
1 large clove garlic, minced
3 tablespoons butter or
  margarine

2 cans (11 ounces each)
  condensed tomato bisque soup
2 soup cans water
2 tablespoons lime juice
1 cup green pepper strips

In large saucepan, brown lamb and mushrooms and cook eggplant with garlic in butter. Blend in soups, water, and lime juice. Bring to boil; reduce heat. Cover; simmer 15 minutes. Add green pepper. Cook 15 minutes more or until done. Stir occasionally. Makes about 7 1/2 cups.

GUACAMOLE SOUP

Garnish this lightly spiced tomato soup with a mound of mashed avocado, lemon juice and whipped cream. If questions come up about an unusual taste, it's tequila.

1 tablespoon finely chopped
  onion
1 small clove garlic, minced
2 teaspoons chili powder
1 tablespoon butter or
  margarine
1 can (10 3/4 ounces) condensed
  tomato soup

1 soup can water
1 to 2 tablespoons tequila
1 small ripe avocado, mashed
2 teaspoons lemon juice
1/8 teaspoon salt
1/4 cup heavy cream, whipped

In saucepan, cook onion with garlic and chili powder in butter until tender. Add soup, water, and tequila. Heat; stir occasionally. Meanwhile, combine avocado, lemon juice, and salt. Fold in whipped cream. Serve as garnish for soup. Makes about 2 1/2 cups.

ALPINE CHEESE SOUP

The piquant flavor of this asparagus-cheese soup is attributed to the addition of beer.

2 cans (10 3/4 ounces each)
  condensed cream of shrimp
  soup
1/2 teaspoon dry mustard
1 1/2 soup cans milk

1 bottle (8 fl. oz.) beer
1 teaspoon Worcestershire
1 package (10 ounces) frozen cut
  asparagus
2 cups shredded Swiss cheese

In saucepan, blend soup and mustard; add milk, beer, Worcestershire, and asparagus. Bring to boil; cover. Reduce heat; simmer 15 minutes or until done. Add cheese; heat until cheese melts. Stir occasionally. Makes about 7 1/2 cups.

VELVET MUSHROOM POTAGE

An elegant soup to serve when you want to impress a very important person . . . or two.

1/4 cup shredded carrot
1/4 cup chopped celery
2 tablespoons butter or
   margarine
1 can (10 3/4 ounces) condensed
   cream of mushroom soup

1/4 pound chopped fresh
   mushrooms (about 1 1/3 cups)
3/4 cup light cream
3 tablespoons chablis or other
   dry white wine

In saucepan, cook carrot and celery in butter until tender. Add soup and mushrooms. Pour into blender; blend until smooth. Return mixture to saucepan; gradually stir in cream and wine. Heat; stir occasionally. Garnish with additional shredded carrot. Makes about 3 cups.

SAUERBRATEN SOUP WITH DUMPLINGS

Create a wonderfully different soup for the men in your house. The meat, soup and other ingredients marinate, then come to a boil, and are topped with dumplings.

1 pound boneless sirloin
   steak (1-inch thick)
2 cans (10 1/2 ounces each)
   condensed onion soup
1/4 cup red wine vinegar
1/8 teaspoon ground ginger
Generous dash ground allspice
6 whole cloves
3 medium potatoes, cooked,
   mashed, and chilled
   (about 1 pound)

1 egg, slightly beaten
1 teaspoon dried dill weed, crushed
1/2 teaspoon salt
1/2 cup flour
3 soup cans water
2 tablespoons cornstarch
1/2 cup sour cream

Freeze meat 1 hour to firm (makes slicing easier); slice into thin strips. To make marinade, in bowl, blend 1 can soup, wine vinegar, ginger, allspice, and cloves; add meat. Marinate in refrigerator 8 hours or more; stir occasionally. Meanwhile, to make dumplings, combine potatoes, egg, dill, salt, and flour. On lightly floured board, shape into 14 balls (1 1/2 inch). In large saucepan, combine remaining soup, water, cornstarch, marinade, and meat. Bring to boil, stirring until thickened. Drop dumplings into simmering soup. Cover; simmer 10 minutes. Stir occasionally. Gradually blend about 1 cup hot soup into sour cream. Slowly stir sour cream mixture into soup. Makes about 8 cups.

UKRAINIAN BORSCHT

A grand old soup in European tradition—the meat course is included.

2 cans (11 1/2 ounces each)
   condensed bean with bacon
   soup
2 soup cans water
4 smoked pork chops (about
   1 pound)
4 cups cabbage cut in long
   thin shreds

2 cups fresh beets cut in
   thin strips
1 cup sliced celery
1/2 cup chopped fresh tomatoes
2 medium onions, quartered
1 large potato, diced
   (about 1 cup)

In large saucepan, combine ingredients. Bring to boil; reduce heat. Cover; cook over low heat 30 minutes. Stir occasionally. Makes about 9 1/2 cups.

OLD FASHIONED VEGETABLE SOUP

Cubed beef and cabbage team up with a variety of vegetables to make a robust soup for a cold winter evening.

1 can (10 1/2 ounces) condensed
   beef broth
1 can (10 1/2 ounces) condensed
   vegetable soup
2 soup cans water
2 cups cabbage cut in long
   thin shreds
1 cup cubed cooked beef

1 can (about 8 ounces) tomatoes,
   cut up
1/2 cup uncooked small shell macaroni
1 medium onion, sliced
2 tablespoons grated Parmesan
   cheese
1 medium clove garlic, minced
1/2 teaspoon caraway seed

In large saucepan, combine ingredients. Bring to boil; reduce heat. Simmer 30 minutes or until done; stir occasionally. Makes about 8 1/2 cups.

PETITE MARMITE

In France this soup takes a day to prepare. But you can have it from saucepan to soup plate in less than one hour.

1/2 pound boneless round
   steak (1-inch thick)
1 pound chicken parts
5 small turnips (about 1/2
   pound), quartered
1 cup chopped celery

1 medium bay leaf
2 1/2 cups water
2 cans (10 1/2 ounces each)
   condensed chicken with rice soup
1/2 cup sliced green onions
1 cup diagonally sliced carrots

Cut meat in 1-inch cubes. In large saucepan, combine beef, chicken, turnips, celery, bay, and water. Bring to boil; cover. Reduce heat; simmer 30 minutes. Add soup, onions, and carrots; cook 15 minutes more or until done. Stir occasionally. Skim off fat. Makes about 9 1/2 cups.

ISLAND BEAN SOUP

Bring the flavor of Cuba to your table with this version of their traditional black bean soup.

1/2 pound boneless top round
  steak, diced
1/2 cup chopped carrots
1/2 cup chopped onion
1/4 pound salt pork, diced
  (2/3 cup)

2 cans (11 ounces each) condensed
  black bean soup
2 soup cans water
1/2 cup Port or other sweet
  red wine
Generous dash cayenne pepper

In large saucepan, brown beef and cook carrots and onion with salt pork until tender. Blend in remaining ingredients. Bring to boil; cover. Reduce heat; simmer 30 minutes. Stir occasionally. Garnish with lemon slices. Makes about 7 cups.

CHILLED VEGETABLE POTAGE

Serve in crockery bowls accompanied by rye melba toast or pumpernickel rounds.

1/2 cup shredded cabbage
1/2 cup shredded carrot
1/4 teaspoon caraway seed
2 tablespoons butter or
  margarine

1 can (11 1/4 ounces) condensed
  green pea soup
1/4 cup sour cream
1 soup can water

In saucepan, cook cabbage and carrot with caraway in butter until tender. Add soup and sour cream; gradually stir in water. Heat; stir occasionally. Pour into blender; blend until smooth. Chill 6 hours or more. Makes about 3 1/2 cups.

RUBY ORANGE SOUP

Beets and oranges have an affinity for each other. Heat them in beef broth, ladle into a serving bowl and chill several hours. An orange slice garnish is perfect.

1 can (about 16 ounces) sliced
  beets
1 can (10 1/2 ounces) condensed
  beef broth

1/2 cup orange juice
1 teaspoon grated orange rind

Drain beets, reserving juice. Cut beets in thin strips. In saucepan, combine beets, beet juice, broth, orange juice, and rind. Heat; stir occasionally. Chill 6 hours or more. Garnish with orange slices. Makes about 3 1/2 cups.

VEGETARIAN YOGURT SOUP

Anyone who thinks a vegetarian exists on dull food is mistaken. This recipe proves otherwise. Yogurt and eggs provide protein.

2 tablespoons chopped onion
1/2 teaspoon marjoram leaves, crushed
2 tablespoons butter or margarine
2 cans (10 3/4 ounces each) condensed cream of asparagus soup

1 cup plain yogurt
1 1/2 soup cans water
1/4 teaspoon garlic salt
4 hard-cooked eggs, chopped
1 cup bean sprouts
1 cup cooked rice

In large saucepan, cook onion with marjoram in butter until tender. Blend in soup, yogurt, water, and garlic salt. Add remaining ingredients. Heat; stir occasionally. Makes about 7 cups.

ICE CAP VICHYSSOISE

If you've been meaning to make this classic cold soup use the contemporary method by combining chicken broth and cream of potato soup. Garnish with green onions.

1 can (10 3/4 ounces) condensed chicken broth
1 can (10 3/4 ounces) condensed cream of potato soup

1 soup can milk
1 package (8 ounces) cream cheese, softened
2 tablespoons sliced green onions

In electric blender, combine ingredients; blend until smooth. Pour into saucepan. Heat; stir occasionally. Chill overnight. Makes about 5 cups.

FRESH ASPARAGUS PUREE

Garnish this cold asparagus-potato soup with lemon slices (notched if you like) and deep green watercress sprigs. Lovely to look at; even better to eat.

1 pound fresh asparagus, cut in 2-inch pieces
1 medium onion, thickly sliced
2 cans (10 3/4 ounces each) condensed cream of potato soup

1 soup can milk
1 soup can water
1 tablespoon lemon juice
1/2 teaspoon celery salt
Generous dash pepper

In saucepan, cook asparagus and onion in water 10 minutes or until tender; drain. Stir in soup, milk, 1 soup can water, lemon juice, and seasonings. Heat; stir occasionally. In electric blender, blend soup mixture, a little at a time, until smooth. Chill 6 hours or more. Thin to desired consistency with additional milk. Garnish with lemon slices and watercress. Makes about 6 1/2 cups.

SQUASH BISQUE

An unusual bisque made from fall squash and apples with a mushroom soup base. Since rosemary stands for remembrance, you must add its leaves for lingering flavor.

3 cups diced butternut squash
1 1/2 cups chopped tart apples
1/2 cup chopped onion
1/8 teaspoon rosemary leaves, crushed
1 cup water
2 cans (10 3/4 ounces each) condensed cream of mushroom soup

1 soup can milk
Generous dash grated orange rind
Generous dash pepper
1 1/2 cups cooked chicken cut in strips

In large saucepan, combine squash, apples, onion, rosemary, and water. Bring to boil; cover. Reduce heat; simmer 20 minutes or until done. Stir in soup, milk, orange rind, and pepper. Blend in electric blender, a little at a time, until smooth. Return to saucepan; add chicken. Heat; stir occasionally. Garnish with additional orange rind. Makes about 8 cups.

CHILLED CRANBERRY TOMATO PARFAIT

Today's glassware lends itself beautifully to a swirled soup. Serve it in parfait or whiskey sour glasses.

1 can (10 3/4 ounces) condensed tomato soup
1/2 soup can cranberry juice

1/2 soup can water
1 teaspoon lemon juice
Sour cream

In saucepan, combine all ingredients except sour cream. Heat; stir occasionally. Chill 6 hours or more. In glasses, swirl sour cream through soup. Makes about 2 1/2 cups.

CUCUMBER A LA CREME

Small balloon-type, well-chilled wine glasses make perfect "bowls" for this lightly seasoned cold cucumber soup.

2 cups diced peeled cucumbers
1/3 cup finely chopped green onions
1 tablespoon chopped parsley
1/8 teaspoon dried dill weed
1/8 teaspoon ground mace
1/8 teaspoon sugar
3 tablespoons butter or margarine
1 can (10 3/4 ounces) condensed chicken broth
2 tablespoons flour
1/2 cup light cream

In saucepan, cook cucumber and onions with parsley, dill, mace, and sugar in butter until tender. Meanwhile, gradually stir broth into flour until smooth; add to cucumber mixture. Heat, stirring until thickened. Pour into blender; blend until smooth. Stir in cream. Chill 6 hours or more. Thin to desired consistency with additional cream. Garnish with cucumber slices. Makes about 3 1/2 cups.

SOUTHERN STYLE VEGETABLE SOUP

Give pork hocks and collard greens a chance to prove themselves flavorful in each bowl of this good soup. Serve with hot biscuits.

3 smoked pork hocks (about 2 pounds)
2 cans (11 1/4 ounces each) condensed green pea soup
1 can (10 1/2 ounces) condensed old fashioned vegetable soup
3 soup cans water
1 package (9 ounces) frozen chopped collard greens
1/4 cup chopped onion
1/4 teaspoon cayenne pepper

In large heavy pan, cover hocks with water. Bring to boil; cover. Reduce heat; simmer 1 hour. Drain. Blend in soup; gradually stir in 3 soup cans water. Add remaining ingredients. Simmer 2 hours. Stir occasionally. Makes about 6 cups.

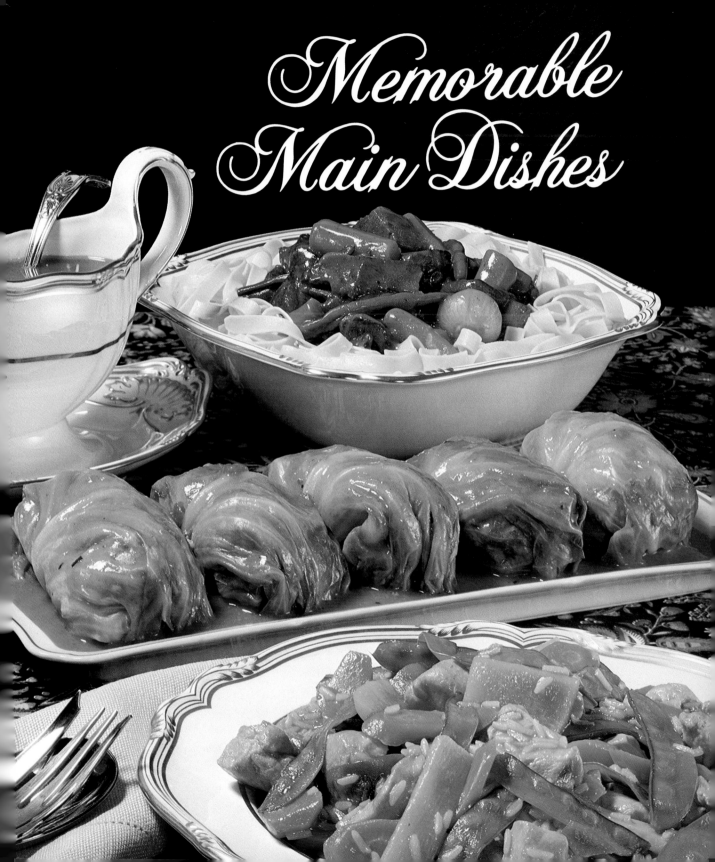

Memorable Main Dishes

Memorable Main Dishes

Like a major theme in music, the main course dominates and sets the tone for a menu whatever its style. Whether the occasion is with candlelight on the patio, a buffet for colleagues, or a more formal event, the main course is the major theme and all other courses revolve as satellites around it.

Historically, this was not always so, but in today's world which is so open to new ideas and lifestyles, the main course is truly a challenge in creativity. Why cook an ordinary baked ham when a Fruited Caribbean Ham can provide more creative satisfaction and a new taste adventure. Choosing an impressive or unusual dish around which a menu is planned also provides an opportunity to use other imaginative elements.

As the photograph suggests, main course possibilities, ranging from a Shanghai Chicken and Vegetables to a Hungarian Pork Roast, can be dramatic and almost endless in variation.

Yet, the ingredients need not be esoteric. What all the dishes in this section have in common is that condensed soups are used to make preparation easier and to help blend the distinctive flavors of all the ingredients in the recipes.

Veal Mediterranean, delicious to look at, has the flavors of artichokes and mushroom with tangy seasonings indigenous to the warm Italian climate. Succulent Stuffed Cabbage Rolls steeped in flavors of beef, sausage, cabbage and herbs are a marvelous choice for a brisk winter dinner. Hungarian Pork Roast simmered with paprika and other seasonings is a distinctive and sophisticated treatment of pork loin. The tender Beef Ragout can be made in a third of the time of its old-fashioned counter part, yet is at least its equal in all respects.

America, historically, has had an abundance of food. Early settlers were astounded at the partridges, turkey, and other wild life along the East Coast. Lobsters were so plentiful in New England that Governor Bradford, in the early 1600's, apologized that his colony was short of other food. To this natural abundance came an enormous influx of nationalities and cultures.

Immigrants who came to America during the 1800's and 1900's brought with them a wide range of food tastes, preferences and skills. Family recipes and cooking techniques were quickly transplanted and sometimes adapted to take advantage of local food supplies. Along with these ethnic treasures, which are still part of our eating patterns, regional specialties evolved in a similar fashion.

48

Today, this rich food heritage is most evident in what is called the "main course" because this is the center around which meals are structured and the area where most people look for inspiration, variety and uniqueness.

The evolution of the main meal and thus of the main course has seen many changes over the centuries. Very early man ate whenever food was available, whenever woman, the food gatherer, was successful. Greeks and Romans generally ate two meals a day, a light one at midday and a main meal in mid or late afternoon.

By Chaucer's time, England and the European continent had adopted the custom of eating the main meal in the morning, and Frenchmen were known to rise before dawn to eat their big meal of the day at 9 a.m. Later, England's number of meals consisted of four, the last actually comprising a generous late evening snack.

Many main courses were featured at medieval tables and all were placed in the center of the table at the same time. Lesser dishes were arranged on the side, giving rise to their name, "side dishes." It was not until the 16th century that "courses" in the meal came into vogue, giving some order to the menu.

Feasting was prevalent among the privileged at this time and banquets provided an arena for spectacular productions. By the reign of Louis XIV, a time of great culinary achievement, it was customary to dine on the main meal at 10 p.m. Victorian era diners in England enjoyed their main meal mid-evening, giving rise to a substantial luncheon and afternoon tea.

Twentieth century America has seen changes in meal patterns. As we moved from being predominantly an agricultural society to an urban one, our main meal changed from noon time to the evening. Try some of the recipes in the following chapter to add pleasure to that eating occasion.

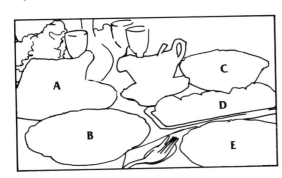

A HUNGARIAN PORK ROAST
B VEAL MEDITERRANEAN
C BEEF RAGOUT
D STUFFED CABBAGE ROLLS
E SHANGHAI CHICKEN AND VEGETABLES

BARBECUED SPARERIBS

Succulent ribs appeal to all age groups. Ground cloves perk up the sauce in which these ribs are baked.

6 pounds spareribs, cut in
    serving-size pieces
1/2 cup chopped onion
2 tablespoons butter or
    margarine
2 cans (10 3/4 ounces each)
    condensed tomato soup

1/2 cup brown sugar
1/3 cup Worcestershire
1/4 cup hot sauce
1 tablespoon prepared mustard
1 tablespoon vinegar
1/4 teaspoon ground cloves

In large pan, cover spareribs with water. Simmer 1 hour; drain. Arrange in single layer in two 2 1/2-quart shallow baking dishes (13x9x2"). Meanwhile, in saucepan, cook onion in butter until tender. Stir in remaining ingredients. Simmer 5 minutes; stir often. Spoon over spareribs. Bake at 450°F. for 30 minutes or until done. Makes 6 servings.

GLAZED ROLLED LEG OF LAMB

Orange marmalade glazes and flavors the lamb. Pass gravy made from golden mushroom soup and mint leaves. The lamb and you will love it.

4-pound leg of lamb, boned
    and rolled
2 tablespoons orange marmalade
1 can (10 3/4 ounces) condensed
    golden mushroom soup

1/4 cup water
1 teaspoon dried mint leaves,
    crushed

In shallow roasting pan, place lamb fat-side up on rack. Roast at 325°F. about 2 hours or until done (30 to 35 minutes per pound or 175°F. on meat thermometer). Spread marmalade on meat last 30 minutes of roasting. Remove lamb; keep warm. Spoon off fat, saving drippings. On top of range, in roasting pan, stir remaining ingredients into drippings. Heat, stirring to loosen browned bits. Serve with lamb. Makes 4 to 6 servings.

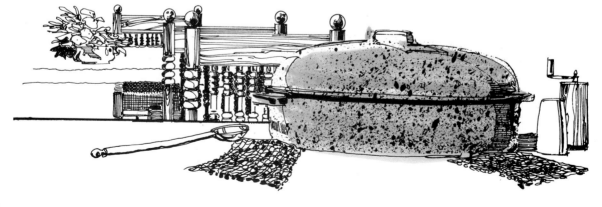

TAMALE BAKE

Cornmeal or "masa" is truly Mexican. Here, the cornmeal bakes as a topping over a meat and vegetable combination.

1 pound ground beef
1/4 pound pork sausage
1/2 cup chopped onion
1 can (10 3/4 ounces) condensed
   tomato soup
1/2 cup water
1 can (about 8 ounces) whole
   kernel golden corn, undrained
1/3 cup sliced ripe olives

1 to 2 tablespoons chili powder
1 tablespoon chopped Jalapeño
   peppers
Generous dash crushed red pepper
4 cups water
1 cup cornmeal
1 teaspoon salt
1 cup shredded sharp Cheddar cheese

In skillet, brown beef and cook sausage and onion until done. Stir to separate meat; pour off fat. Add soup, water, corn, olives, chili powder, Jalapeño peppers, and red pepper. Heat; stir occasionally. Meanwhile, bring 3 cups water to boil. Combine cornmeal, salt, and 1 cup <u>cold</u> water; pour into boiling water, stirring constantly. Bring to boil, stirring. Cover; cook over low heat 5 minutes. Stir often. Pour hot soup mixture into 2-quart shallow baking dish (12x8x2"); spread with cornmeal mixture. Bake at 350°F. for 15 minutes; sprinkle with cheese. Bake 15 minutes more. Spoon off fat before serving. Makes 6 servings.

PINTO BEANS WITH PORK HOCKS

Those who live outside the south, take heed. Pinto beans and well seasoned pork hocks make a hearty, economical meal.

1 cup dried pinto beans
1 teaspoon salt
2 cups water
3 smoked pork hocks
   (about 3/4 pound each)
1 large onion, thickly sliced
1 teaspoon marjoram leaves,
   crushed

1 can (10 3/4 ounces) condensed
   tomato soup
1/4 cup chopped parsley
1 medium clove garlic, minced
1/8 teaspoon cayenne pepper

Combine beans, salt, and water; soak overnight. Drain. In large heavy pan, cover pork hocks with water; add onion and marjoram leaves. Bring to boil; reduce heat. Simmer 1 hour 30 minutes. Drain, reserving liquid. Add 3 cups reserved liquid, beans, and remaining ingredients. Cover; cook over low heat 2 hours or until done. Stir occasionally. Add more reserved liquid if necessary. Makes 3 servings.

2 ALARM CHILI

Mexican cooking crosses the border in this hot chili. While the mixture itself is beanless, you can serve it with rice or pinto beans.

1 1/2 pounds boneless chuck, cut into 1/2-inch cubes
2 tablespoons salad oil
1 can (10 1/2 ounces) condensed beef broth
1/2 soup can water
1 cup chopped onion
1 large clove garlic, minced
2 large bay leaves, crushed
1 tablespoon ground cumin seed
1 tablespoon oregano leaves, crushed

1 tablespoon paprika
1/4 teaspoon salt
Generous dash crushed red pepper
1 can (about 16 ounces) tomatoes, cut up
2 tablespoons chopped Jalapeño peppers
2 tablespoons cornmeal
Cooked rice or pinto beans

In large saucepan, brown beef in oil. Stir in broth, water, onion, garlic, and seasonings. Cover; cook over low heat 1 hour 30 minutes. Add tomatoes, Jalapeño peppers, and cornmeal. Cook 30 minutes more or until done. Stir occasionally. Serve over rice. Makes about 4 cups.

ALBONDIGAS

Albondigas . . . these are Mexican meatballs—moist, spicy and delicious. Traditionally they are served with rice and beans.

1/2 pound ground beef
1/2 pound ground pork
1 egg, slightly beaten
2 tablespoons fine dry bread crumbs
1/4 teaspoon salt
Dash pepper
1 large clove garlic, minced
2 teaspoons chili powder

1/2 teaspoon oregano leaves, crushed
1 tablespoon shortening
1 can (10 3/4 ounces) condensed tomato soup
1/2 cup water
1/3 cup finely chopped onion
Cooked rice

Combine beef, pork, egg, bread crumbs, salt, and pepper. Shape into 16 meatballs. In skillet, brown meatballs with garlic, chili powder, and oregano in shortening. Stir in soup, water, and onion. Cover; cook over low heat 20 minutes or until done. Stir occasionally. Serve over rice. Makes about 3 1/2 cups.

SPINACH MEATBALLS

Having problems getting spinach into your family's meals? Incorporate it into meatballs made succulent with soup and seasonings.

2 cans (10 3/4 ounces each)
  condensed tomato soup
1 pound ground beef
3/4 cup cooked well-drained
  chopped spinach
1 egg, slightly beaten
1/4 cup finely chopped onion

1/2 teaspoon salt
1/8 teaspoon pepper
2 tablespoons shortening
1/2 cup water
1 teaspoon oregano leaves, crushed
Cooked spaghetti
Grated Parmesan cheese

Mix <u>thoroughly</u> 1/4 cup soup, beef, spinach, egg, onion, salt, and pepper; shape <u>firmly</u> into 16 meatballs. In skillet, brown meatballs in shortening; pour off fat. Add remaining soup, water, and oregano. Cover; cook over low heat 20 minutes or until done. Stir occasionally. Serve over cooked spaghetti with Parmesan cheese. Makes about 4 1/2 cups.

BEEF STUFFED SQUASH

Green and gold rimmed squash shells form individual casseroles for a tomato soup-beef combination topped with cheese.

6 medium acorn squash
  (about 1 pound each)
1 can (10 3/4 ounces) condensed
  tomato soup
1 pound ground beef
1/2 cup fine dry bread crumbs
1/2 cup grated Parmesan cheese

1 egg, slightly beaten
1/2 cup finely chopped celery
1/2 cup finely chopped onion
1 small clove garlic, minced
4 slices (about 4 ounces) sharp
  process cheese, cut into 12 strips

Cut a 1-inch slice off top of each squash; remove seeds and fibers. Cook squash in boiling water 10 minutes; remove and drain. Place squash upright in a 2 1/2-quart shallow baking dish (13x9x2"). Combine remaining ingredients except cheese; spoon into squash. Bake at 350°F. for 1 hour 15 minutes or until done. Top with cheese; bake until cheese melts. Makes 6 servings.

BAVARIAN PORK AND CABBAGE

In southern Germany pork and cabbage are flavored with onion and caraway seed. This hearty dish could be accompanied by thick slices of rye bread.

4 thick pork chops (about
  2 1/2 pounds)
1 can (10 3/4 ounces) condensed
  cream of mushroom soup
1/4 cup milk
1/2 cup chopped onion
1/2 teaspoon caraway seed

1/8 teaspoon salt
Generous dash pepper
1 small head cabbage (about
  1 pound), cut in 4 wedges
2 cups sliced carrots
1 cup sliced celery

In skillet, brown chops (use shortening if necessary); pour off fat. Stir in soup, milk, onion, and seasonings. Cover; cook over low heat 25 minutes. Add vegetables; cook 20 minutes more or until done. Stir occasionally. Uncover; cook to desired consistency. Makes 4 servings.

SZECHWAN BEEF

Natives of this area of China like their food well spiced. Serve rice with the beef to mellow the spicy flavor.

1 pound boneless chuck roast
  (about 2-inches thick)
1 egg white
3 tablespoons cornstarch
1 cup diagonally sliced
  green onions
1 teaspoon crushed red pepper
2 medium cloves garlic, minced
1/8 teaspoon ground ginger

2 tablespoons salad oil
1 can (10 1/2 ounces) condensed
  beef broth
1/2 cup sliced radishes
2 tablespoons ketchup
2 tablespoons sherry
2 teaspoons soy sauce
Cooked rice

Freeze meat 1 hour to firm (makes slicing easier); slice into very thin strips. In small bowl, beat egg white until stiff peaks form, gradually adding 2 tablespoons cornstarch. Dip beef in egg white mixture. Fry, a few strips at a time, in deep fat at 350°F. until browned. Drain on absorbent towels. Meanwhile, in saucepan, cook onions with pepper, garlic, and ginger in oil until just tender. Add beef strips, broth, radishes, remaining cornstarch, ketchup, sherry, and soy sauce. Cook, stirring until thickened. Serve with rice. Makes 3 cups.

SAUERBRATEN

Ideal for the working wife who loves to entertain on weekends. The meat marinates in the refrigerator for 3 days before cooking for company.

4-pound boneless chuck roast (about 2 inches thick)
1 can (10 1/2 ounces) condensed beef broth
1 cup vinegar
12 whole peppercorns
4 whole cloves
2 medium bay leaves
1 1/2 teaspoons salt

1/4 teaspoon pepper
2 tablespoons shortening
4 medium carrots, cut in 2-inch pieces (about 1/2 pound)
4 medium onions, sliced
3/4 cup crushed gingersnaps (about 12)
1/2 cup water
1 tablespoon sugar

Place meat in large bowl. To make marinade, in saucepan, combine broth, vinegar, and seasonings. Heat to boiling; cool. Pour over meat; cover and refrigerate. Marinate 3 days, turning meat once a day. Remove meat from marinade; drain. Strain marinade and reserve. In large heavy pan, brown meat in shortening; pour off fat. Add reserved marinade, carrots, and onions. Cover; cook over low heat 2 hours or until done. Stir occasionally. Remove meat and carrots; keep warm. Stir gingersnaps, water, and sugar into sauce. Cook over low heat 10 minutes or until thickened, stirring until sauce is smooth. Serve with meat and carrots. Makes 8 servings.

MIDDLE EAST LEG OF LAMB

Lamb has an affinity for garlic. Insert small pieces into slits made in the lamb with a sharp knife. As the leg roasts, the garlic permeates its juices.

6-pound leg of lamb
1 medium clove garlic, sliced
1/4 teaspoon salt
1/8 teaspoon pepper

1 can (10 3/4 ounces) condensed cream of chicken soup
2 tablespoons currant jelly
1/2 cup water
1 tablespoon chopped parsley

Remove fell from lamb (parchment-like covering); trim excess fat. Cut small slits in lamb; insert garlic. Season with salt and pepper. In shallow roasting pan, place lamb fat-side up on rack. Roast at 325°F. for about 3 hours or until done (30 to 35 minutes per pound or until 175°F. on meat thermometer). Remove lamb; keep warm. Spoon off fat, saving drippings. On top of range, in roasting pan, stir remaining ingredients into drippings. Heat, stirring to loosen browned bits. Serve with lamb. Makes 6 to 8 servings.

STUFFED CABBAGE ROLLS

A favorite meal of people in the Balkan and mid-eastern countries. Cinnamon and basil make our version unusual.

8 large cabbage leaves
1 can (11 ounces) condensed tomato bisque soup
1 pound ground beef
1/2 pound pork sausage, cooked and drained

1/4 cup chopped onion
1 cup cooked rice
1 egg, slightly beaten
1/2 teaspoon salt
1/8 teaspoon ground cinnamon
1/8 teaspoon basil leaves, crushed

Cook cabbage leaves in boiling salted water a few minutes to soften; drain. Mix thoroughly 2 tablespoons soup and remaining ingredients except basil. Divide meat mixture among cabbage leaves; roll up, folding in edges (secure with toothpicks if necessary). In skillet, blend remaining soup and basil. Place rolls seam-side down in soup mixture. Cover; cook over low heat 40 minutes or until done. Stir occasionally, spooning sauce over rolls. Uncover; cook to desired consistency. Makes 4 servings.

VEAL MEDITERRANEAN

White wine, artichoke hearts, olives and capers blend beautifully with veal.

1 1/2 pounds veal cubes (1 inch)
2 tablespoons olive oil
1 can (10 3/4 ounces) condensed tomato soup
1/2 cup chablis or other dry white wine
1/4 cup water
2 medium cloves garlic, minced

1 package (9 ounces) frozen artichoke hearts
2 cups sliced fresh mushrooms (about 1/2 pound)
4 slices (about 4 ounces) salami, cut in strips
1/2 cup pitted ripe olives
2 tablespoons drained capers

In large heavy pan, brown veal in oil. Add soup, wine, water, and garlic. Cover; cook over low heat 45 minutes. Add remaining ingredients. Cook 15 minutes more or until done. Stir occasionally. Makes about 5 1/2 cups

MINI-MEAT LOAVES

Keep utility bills low. Brown and cook individual meat loaves in a skillet in less than a half hour.

1 can (10 3/4 ounces) condensed tomato soup	1 teaspoon salt
2 pounds ground beef	1/4 teaspoon pepper
1/4 cup fine dry bread crumbs	1/4 teaspoon rubbed sage
1 egg, slightly beaten	1/4 teaspoon thyme leaves, crushed
1/4 cup finely chopped onion	2 tablespoons shortening
	2 to 4 tablespoons water

Mix <u>thoroughly</u> 1/4 cup soup, beef, bread crumbs, egg, onion, salt, and 1/8 teaspoon <u>each</u> pepper, sage, and thyme. Shape <u>firmly</u> into 6 mini-meat loaves. In skillet, brown loaves in shortening; pour off fat. Stir in remaining soup and seasonings and water. Cover; cook over low heat 20 minutes or until done. Stir occasionally. Makes 6 servings.

CALF'S LIVER SAUTE

Bacon and liver are teammates. Saute this tender meat, then add a wine-onion soup mixture to sauce it.

4 slices bacon	1 tablespoon flour
1 pound calf's liver	1 cup sliced cooked carrots
1/4 cup Burgundy or other dry red wine	1 small bay leaf
1 can (10 1/2 ounces) condensed onion soup	1/8 teaspoon thyme leaves, crushed

In skillet, cook bacon until crisp; remove and crumble. Pour off all but 2 tablespoons drippings; brown liver in drippings. Add wine, stirring to loosen browned bits. Gradually blend soup into flour until smooth; slowly stir into wine. Add bacon and remaining ingredients. Cover; cook over low heat for 10 minutes or until done. Stir occasionally. Garnish with parsley. Makes 4 servings.

HUNGARIAN PORK ROAST

Paprika—a traditional Hungarian spice seasons this pork roast to perfection.

3 to 4-pound pork loin rib roast	1/2 cup chopped onion
2 tablespoons shortening	1 tablespoon paprika
1 can (10 3/4 ounces) condensed golden mushroom soup	1 medium bay leaf
1/2 cup water	1/2 teaspoon salt
	Dash pepper

In large heavy pan, brown meat in shortening; pour off fat. Add soup, water, onion, and seasonings. Cover; cook over low heat 2 hours 15 minutes or until done. Stir occasionally. Remove bay leaf. Thicken sauce if desired. Makes 4 to 6 servings.

CARAWAY PORK RAGOUT

A true ragout with meat cut in regular shapes and sizes, browned and accompanied by vegetables.

1 1/2 pounds well-trimmed boneless pork loin, cut in 1-inch cubes	1 cup chopped onion
2 tablespoons shortening	1/2 teaspoon caraway seed
1 can (11 ounces) condensed Cheddar cheese soup	2 cups broccoli flowerets
1 can (10 3/4 ounces) condensed chicken broth	2 cups cauliflowerets
	3/4 cup sweet vermouth
	3 tablespoons flour
	Cooked noodles

In large heavy pan, brown pork in shortening; pour off fat. Stir in soups, onion, and caraway. Cover; cook over low heat 1 hour 30 minutes. Add broccoli, cauliflowerets, and 1/2 cup vermouth. Cover; cook over low heat 30 minutes more or until done. Stir occasionally. Gradually blend remaining vermouth into flour until smooth; slowly stir into sauce. Cook, stirring until thickened. Serve with noodles. Makes about 7 cups.

BEEF BOURGUIGNONNE

An up-to-date version of this classic French dish with red wine is easily made with mushroom soup. Its name is derived from the Burgundy region.

2 slices bacon	1 medium bay leaf
1 1/2 pounds beef cubes (about 1 1/2 inches)	2 tablespoons chopped parsley
1 can (10 3/4 ounces) condensed golden mushroom soup	1/4 teaspoon thyme leaves, crushed
1/3 cup Burgundy or other dry red wine	1 pound small whole white onions (about 16)
1 large clove garlic, minced	Cooked noodles

In skillet, cook bacon until crisp; remove and crumble. Brown beef in drippings. Add soup, wine, garlic, bay, parsley, thyme, and bacon. Cover; cook over low heat 1 hour. Add onions; cook 1 hour more or until done. Stir occasionally. Remove bay leaf. Serve over noodles. Makes about 4 1/2 cups.

FONDUE TERIYAKI

Honey, with its natural sweetness, rounds out the flavor of this simple-to-make marinade.

1 1/2 pounds well-trimmed boneless sirloin steak (1-inch thick)	1/4 cup soy sauce
	1/4 cup finely chopped onion
	1 large clove garlic, minced
1 can (10 1/2 ounces) condensed consomme	1 tablespoon honey
	1 tablespoon cornstarch
1/4 cup sherry	Salad oil

Freeze meat 1 hour to firm (makes slicing easier); slice into <u>very</u> thin strips. To make marinade, combine consomme, sherry, soy, onion, garlic, and honey; pour over steak. Marinate 1 hour or more. Remove steak from marinade; drain. In saucepan, combine marinade and cornstarch. Cook, stirring until thickened. Meanwhile, half-fill fondue pot with oil; heat until oil is gently bubbling. Thread meat on fondue forks. Cook until desired doneness. Serve with marinade. Makes 4 servings.

MEATLOAF A LA ROMA

Take a tip from the Italian people. Add chopped salami to spice the ground beef for this meat loaf.

1 can (10 3/4 ounces) condensed golden mushroom soup	1 egg, slightly beaten
	1 large clove garlic, minced
1 1/2 pounds ground beef	Cheese slices cut in triangles
1/2 pound chopped salami	1/2 cup water
1/2 cup fine dry bread crumbs	2 tablespoons chopped parsley
1/3 cup grated Parmesan cheese	1/8 teaspoon grated lemon rind

Mix <u>thoroughly</u> 1/2 cup soup, beef, salami, bread crumbs, Parmesan cheese, egg, and garlic. Shape <u>firmly</u> into loaf; place in shallow baking pan (13x9x2"). Bake at 375°F. for 1 hour 5 minutes or until done. Arrange cheese on loaf; bake until cheese melts. Remove loaf to serving platter; keep warm. Spoon off fat, saving drippings. On top of range, in baking pan, stir remaining soup, water, parsley, and lemon rind into drippings. Cook, stirring to loosen browned bits. Serve with loaf. Makes 6 to 8 servings.

ONION CHUCK

No need for weeping while peeling onions. They're already in the soup that simmers with the meat.

3 1/2-pound boneless chuck roast (about 1 1/2 inches thick)
2 tablespoons shortening
2 cans (10 1/2 ounces each) condensed cream of onion soup
1 cup milk
5 teaspoons lemon juice

1/2 teaspoon ground nutmeg
1/2 teaspoon salt
Generous dash pepper
6 medium carrots (about 3/4 pound), quartered
6 medium potatoes (about 1 1/2 pounds), quartered

Trim fat from meat; cut in 1 1/2-inch cubes. In large heavy pan, brown meat in shortening; pour off fat. Stir in soup, milk, lemon juice, and seasonings. Cover; cook over low heat 1 hour 30 minutes. Add vegetables. Cook 1 hour more or until done. Stir occasionally. Garnish with parsley and lemon slices. Makes about 7 1/2 cups.

STIR-FRY BEEF WITH VEGETABLES

The preparation of meat and vegetables for a stir-fry dish may seem long. But glance at the cooking time—it's short.

1 pound boneless round steak (3/4-inch thick)
1/2 cup diagonally sliced carrot
1/2 cup diagonally sliced celery
1/2 cup diagonally sliced green onions
1/4 teaspoon ground ginger
2 tablespoons butter or margarine

1 can (10 3/4 ounces) condensed beefy mushroom soup
1 1/2 cups water
1 can (16 ounces) Chinese vegetables, drained
1 tablespoon cornstarch
1 tablespoon soy sauce
1 teaspoon brown sugar
1/2 teaspoon salt

Freeze meat 1 hour to firm (makes slicing easier); slice into <u>very</u> thin strips. In skillet, cook carrot, celery, and onion with ginger in butter until <u>just</u> tender; push to one side. Add meat; cook until color <u>just</u> changes (about 3 to 4 minutes). Add remaining ingredients. Cook, stirring until thickened. Serve over rice with additional soy. Makes about 5 cups.

BEEF RAGOUT

This dish is typical of a "browned" ragout because the meat is cut into even sizes and browned in shortening in a heavy pan.

2 pounds boneless sirloin
  steak (1-inch thick)
2 tablespoons shortening
2 cans (10 3/4 ounces each)
  condensed cream of
  mushroom soup
1/2 cup water
1 tablespoon Worcestershire

6 medium carrots, cut in 2-inch
  pieces
8 small whole white onions
  (about 1/2 pound)
1 package (10 ounces) frozen
  whole green beans
Cooked noodles

Cut meat in 1-inch cubes. In large heavy pan, brown meat in shortening; pour off fat. Add remaining ingredients except beans and noodles. Cover; cook over low heat 45 minutes. Add beans; cook 15 minutes more or until done. Stir occasionally. Thicken sauce if desired. Serve over noodles. Makes about 7 cups.

FRENCH LAMB STEW

The combination of tarragon and lamb is not used often enough. You'll agree after you try this delicious stew.

1 1/2 pounds lamb cubes (about
  1 1/2 inch), well trimmed
2 tablespoons shortening
1 can (10 3/4 ounces) condensed
  golden mushroom soup
1/4 cup water
1/4 cup chablis or other dry
  white wine
2 tablespoons chopped parsley

1 large clove garlic, minced
1/4 teaspoon tarragon leaves,
  crushed
2 cups celery diagonally sliced in
  2-inch pieces
8 small whole white onions
  (about 1/2 pound)
Cooked noodles

In large heavy pan, brown lamb in shortening; pour off fat. Add soup, water, wine, parsley, garlic, tarragon, and celery. Cover; cook over low heat 30 minutes. Add onions; cook 1 hour more or until done. Stir occasionally. Serve with noodles. Makes about 5 cups.

SAVORY SKILLET SIRLOIN

No arguments about who gets which piece of steak . . . not when it's cut into cubes.

1 1/2 pounds well-trimmed
   boneless sirloin steak
   (1-inch thick)
2 tablespoons shortening
1 can (10 3/4 ounces) condensed
   golden mushroom soup

1/2 cup water
2 tablespoons sherry
1 large clove garlic, minced
1 medium bay leaf
1 package (9 ounces) frozen whole
   green beans

Cut meat in 1-inch cubes. In skillet, brown meat in shortening; pour off fat. Add remaining ingredients except beans. Cover; cook over low heat 45 minutes. Add beans; cook 15 minutes more or until done. Stir occasionally. Remove bay leaf. Makes about 4 cups.

GLAZED HAM RING

For an unusual flavor to an old favorite try this rye, pork, ham combination.

1 can (10 1/2 ounces) condensed
   onion soup
1 1/2 pounds ground cooked ham
1 pound ground pork
1 cup soft rye bread crumbs

1 egg, slightly beaten
1/2 cup firmly packed brown sugar
1 tablespoon vinegar
1 teaspoon dry mustard

To make loaf, mix <u>thoroughly</u> 3/4 cup soup, ham, pork, bread crumbs, and eggs. In shallow baking dish (13x9x2"), shape <u>firmly</u> into ring (2-inches high with 4-inch opening). Bake at 350°F. for 1 hour 30 minutes. Meanwhile, to make glaze, in small saucepan, combine remaining soup, brown sugar, vinegar, and mustard. Heat; stir occasionally. Brush loaf often with glaze while baking. Makes 6 servings.

HERBED POT ROAST

Easy and delicious well describes this roast with its savory sauce and colorful vegetables.

4-pound beef eye round roast
2 tablespoons shortening
2 cans (10 3/4 ounces each)
   condensed tomato soup
1/2 teaspoon thyme leaves,
   crushed

1/4 teaspoon marjoram leaves,
   crushed
16 small whole white onions
   (about 1 pound)
6 small carrots (about 1/2 pound),
   cut in 2-inch pieces

Trim fat from meat. In large heavy oven-proof pan, brown meat in shortening; pour off fat. Add soup, thyme, and marjoram. Cover; bake at 350°F. for 1 hour 30 minutes. Add vegetables. Cook 1 hour 30 minutes more or until done; stir occasionally. Thicken sauce if desired. Makes 8 servings.

VEAL ROLLINI

Tender veal cutlets, spread with liverwurst, are rolled, skewered and browned in shortening. Add tomato soup, cheese, garlic, herbs. Serve with rice.

1 1/2 pounds thinly sliced
   veal cutlet
1/2 cup liverwurst (4 ounces)
2 tablespoons shortening
1 can (10 3/4 ounces) condensed
   tomato soup
2 tablespoons grated Parmesan
   cheese

1/4 cup chopped parsley
1 large clove garlic, minced
1 teaspoon oregano leaves,
   crushed
Cooked rice

Cut veal into 6 pieces (5x4"); pound. Spread each piece with liverwurst. Roll up; tuck in ends. Fasten with toothpicks or skewers. In skillet, brown roll-ups in shortening; pour off fat. Add remaining ingredients. Cover; cook over low heat 45 minutes or until done. Stir occasionally. Serve over rice. Makes 6 servings.

MOUSSAKA

Afraid to tackle the Greek entree you've eaten in restaurants? Shop for the ingredients in this recipe, follow the easy directions, and it's Moussaka for dinner.

1 medium eggplant (about
   1 1/2 pounds), cut in
   1/4-inch slices
2 eggs, slightly beaten
1 cup fine dry bread crumbs
Olive oil
1 pound ground lamb or beef
1 1/2 cups chopped onion
1 can (10 3/4 ounces) condensed
   tomato soup

2 tablespoons chopped parsley
1/4 teaspoon salt
Generous dash pepper
1 can (10 3/4 ounces) condensed
   cream of mushroom soup
2 egg yolks, well beaten
1/2 cup shredded Swiss cheese

Dip eggplant in slightly beaten egg, then bread crumbs. Brown in olive oil (add oil as needed); remove. In same skillet, brown lamb and cook onion until tender; stir to separate meat. Pour off fat. Add tomato soup, parsley, salt, and pepper. In 2-quart shallow baking dish (12x8x2"), arrange alternate layers of eggplant and meat mixture, ending with layer of eggplant. Blend mushroom soup and egg yolks; pour over eggplant. Sprinkle with cheese. Bake at 325°F. for 45 minutes. Makes 4 to 6 servings.

BOEUF ET SAUCISSE

Sausage and sweets (potatoes) combine with beef and green beans in an oven stew that needs no watching.

1 pound beef cubes (about
   1 1/2 inches)
1/2 pound mild Italian sausage,
   cut in 2-inch pieces
2 tablespoons shortening
2 cans (10 3/4 ounces each)
   condensed tomato soup

1/4 cup water
1/2 cup chopped onion
1 large clove garlic, minced
1 cup fresh whole green beans
2 cups cubed sweet potatoes

In oven-proof skillet, brown meat and sausage in shortening; pour off fat. Add soup, water, onion, and garlic. Cover; bake at 350°F. for 1 hour 30 minutes. Add beans and potatoes. Bake 1 hour more or until done. Makes about 6 1/2 cups.

LASAGNA

There are as many variations of lasagna in Italy as there are provinces. However, the people of Emilia-Romagna in northeastern Italy lay claim to its invention.

1 pound ground beef
1/2 pound hot Italian sausage,
   casing removed
1 cup chopped onion
2 large cloves garlic, minced
1 tablespoon oregano leaves,
   crushed
2 cans (10 3/4 ounces each)
   condensed tomato soup
1 cup water

1 can (6 ounces) tomato paste
2 cups ricotta cheese
2 eggs, slightly beaten
1/4 cup chopped parsley
9 lasagna noodles (about 1/2 pound),
   cooked and drained
8 slices (about 8 ounces)
   mozzarella cheese, cut in
   half crosswise
1/3 cup grated Parmesan cheese

To make sauce, in saucepan, brown beef and cook sausage and onion with garlic and oregano until done; stir to separate meat. Spoon off fat. Stir in soup, water, and tomato paste. Bring to boil; reduce heat. Simmer 30 minutes; stir occasionally. Meanwhile, combine ricotta cheese, eggs, and parsley. In 3-quart shallow baking dish (13x9x2″), arrange 3 alternate layers of noodles, ricotta cheese mixture, mozzarella cheese, sauce, and Parmesan cheese. Bake at 350°F. for 45 minutes or until hot. Let stand 15 minutes before serving. Makes 8 servings.

LAMB CUBES WITH MUSHROOM SAUCE

Currant jelly, rosemary, golden mushroom soup and onion make a fine foursome to cook with lamb.

3 pounds lamb cubes
  (1 1/2 inch)
2 tablespoons shortening
2 cans (10 3/4 ounces each)
  condensed golden mushroom
  soup
1/2 cup water
1 cup sliced onion

2 tablespoons currant jelly
1/4 teaspoon rosemary leaves,
  crushed
1 package (9 ounces) frozen whole
  green beans
1 large tomato, cut in wedges
Cooked noodles

In large heavy pan, brown lamb in shortening; pour off fat. Add soup, water, onion, jelly, and rosemary. Cover; cook over low heat 1 hour 15 minutes. Add beans; cook 15 minutes more or until done. Stir occasionally. Add tomato. Serve over noodles. Makes about 7 1/2 cups.

SHANGHAI CHICKEN AND VEGETABLES

A Chinese chicken stew with rice, sherry, soy sauce, green onions, bamboo shoots and pea pods... touched with a bit of ginger.

2 whole chicken breasts,
  split, skinned, boned,
  and cut in 2-inch
  pieces (1 pound boneless)
2 tablespoons salad oil
2 cans (10 3/4 ounces each)
  condensed chicken broth
1/2 cup raw regular rice
1/2 cup sherry
2 tablespoons soy sauce

1 large clove garlic, minced
1/4 teaspoon ground ginger
2 cups diagonally sliced carrots
1 cup diagonally sliced green onions
1 can (about 8 ounces) bamboo
  shoots, drained
1 package (6 ounces) frozen
  pea pods
1/2 cup water
3 to 4 tablespoons cornstarch

In skillet, lightly brown chicken in oil. Add broth, rice, sherry, soy, garlic, and ginger. Bring to boil; reduce heat. Cover; simmer 15 minutes. Add carrots, onions, and bamboo shoots. Simmer 5 minutes more or until done. Stir occasionally. Add pea pods. Blend water into cornstarch until smooth; slowly stir into stew. Cook, stirring until thickened. Makes about 7 cups.

HAM CREPES WITH SHRIMP SAUCE

Shrimp soup does double duty. It goes into the crepe filling, then teams with tarragon and sour cream to spoon over the top.

1 can (10 3/4 ounces) condensed cream of shrimp soup
1 1/2 cups finely chopped cooked ham
1 package (10 ounces) frozen chopped broccoli, cooked and well drained
6 crepes
1/2 cup sliced green onions
1/4 teaspoon tarragon leaves, crushed
2 tablespoons butter or margarine
2 tablespoons sour cream

To make filling, in saucepan, combine 1/2 cup soup, ham, and broccoli. Heat, stirring. Spoon about 1/3 cup filling on each crepe; roll up. Arrange seam-side down on serving platter; keep warm. Meanwhile, to make sauce, in saucepan, cook onion with tarragon in butter until tender. Add remaining soup and sour cream. Heat; stir occasionally. Serve over crepes. Makes 3 servings.

SCANDINAVIAN CHICKEN WITH SHRIMP

A perfect party dish because the preparation is done ahead. Just whisk them into the oven 20 minutes before you're ready to eat.

1/4 cup finely chopped green onions
1/2 teaspoon dried dill weed, crushed
4 tablespoons butter or margarine
1 can (10 3/4 ounces) condensed cream of chicken soup
1 1/2 cups finely chopped cooked shrimp (about 3/4 pound)
1/8 teaspoon hot pepper sauce
3 whole chicken breasts, split, skinned, and boned (1 1/2 pounds boneless)
Flour
1 egg, slightly beaten
Finely crushed whole wheat wafers (about 1 cup)
Butter or margarine, melted
1/4 cup chopped cucumber
1/4 cup sour cream
1/4 cup water

To make stuffing: In saucepan, cook 2 tablespoons green onions with dill in 2 tablespoons butter until tender. Lightly toss with 1/4 cup soup, shrimp, and hot pepper sauce. Flatten chicken breasts to 1/4-inch thickness. Place about 1/4 cup stuffing in center of each breast. Tuck in ends; roll tightly. Secure with toothpicks. Dip in flour, then egg, then whole wheat crumbs. Refrigerate 30 minutes or more. Place in baking pan; drizzle with melted butter. Bake at 425°F. for 20 minutes or until done.

To make sauce: In saucepan, cook remaining green onions and cucumber in remaining 2 tablespoons butter until tender. Blend in remaining soup, sour cream, and water. Heat; stir occasionally. Serve with roll-ups. Makes 6 servings.

CHICKEN VERONIQUE

As this top-of-the-range entree simmers in the skillet its aroma entices hungry people to the table. Sauced chicken breasts served on rice are always a best bet.

2 whole chicken breasts, split (about 2 pounds)
1 cup quartered fresh mushrooms (about 1/4 pound)
2 tablespoons butter or margarine
1 can (10 3/4 ounces) condensed cream of chicken soup

1 medium clove garlic, minced
2 tablespoons sauterne or other dry white wine
1/2 cup seedless white grapes cut in half
Cooked rice

In skillet, brown chicken and mushrooms in butter. Add remaining ingredients except grapes and rice. Cover; cook over low heat 30 minutes or until done. Stir occasionally. Add grapes; heat. Serve over rice. Makes 4 servings.

SPANISH CHICKEN

The blend of mushrooms, olives, garlic and green peppers lends a Mediterranean flavor to this chicken.

2 pounds chicken parts
2 cups sliced fresh mushrooms (about 1/2 pound)
2 tablespoons shortening
Salt
Pepper
1 can (10 3/4 ounces) condensed tomato soup

1/4 cup chablis or other dry white wine
1 medium bay leaf
1 medium clove garlic, minced
1 medium green pepper, cut in squares
2 tablespoons sliced pimiento-stuffed olives

In skillet, brown chicken and mushrooms in shortening; pour off fat. Season with salt and pepper. Stir in remaining ingredients. Cover; cook over low heat 45 minutes or until done. Stir occasionally. Remove bay leaf. Makes 4 servings.

CHICKEN DIVAN

This velvet chicken sauce couples with broccoli for a special event.

1 can (10 3/4 ounces) condensed cream of mushroom soup
1/4 cup light cream
1 1/2 cups cubed cooked chicken
2 tablespoons melted butter or margarine
1 tablespoon sherry
1/8 teaspoon ground nutmeg
1 package (10 ounces) frozen broccoli spears, cooked and drained
Grated Parmesan cheese

Combine soup, cream, chicken, butter, sherry, and nutmeg. Arrange broccoli in 1 1/2-quart shallow baking dish (10x6x2"); pour chicken mixture over all. Sprinkle with cheese. Bake at 450°F. for 15 minutes or until hot. Makes 4 servings.

CHICKEN BREASTS ESPAGNOLE

Golden mushroom soup, tomatoes and wine tinged with rosemary sauce this baked chicken.

3 whole chicken breasts, split (about 3 pounds)
2 tablespoons butter or margarine, melted
1 can (10 3/4 ounces) condensed golden mushroom soup
1/2 cup drained chopped canned tomatoes
2 tablespoons Port or other sweet red wine
1/4 teaspoon rosemary leaves, crushed

In 3-quart shallow baking dish (13x9x2"), arrange chicken skin-side down. Drizzle chicken with butter. Bake at 400°F. for 20 minutes. Turn chicken; bake 20 minutes more. Meanwhile, combine remaining ingredients; pour over chicken. Bake 20 minutes more or until done. Makes 6 servings.

SAVANNAH CHICKEN

You don't have to be a Georgian to feel the influence of southern cooking. Chicken baked in cheese soup and wine is garnished with peaches . . . perhaps Georgia's best.

2 pounds chicken parts
2 tablespoons butter or margarine, melted
1 can (11 ounces) condensed Cheddar cheese soup
1/4 cup water
1/4 cup sauterne or other dry white wine
1 small clove garlic, minced
4 canned peach halves
Cranberry-orange relish

In shallow baking dish (12x8x2"), place chicken skin-side down. Drizzle with butter. Bake at 400°F. for 20 minutes. Turn; bake 20 minutes more. Meanwhile, combine soup, water, wine, and garlic. Pour over chicken. Bake 20 minutes more or until done. Fill peach center with cranberry-orange relish. Serve with chicken. Makes 4 servings.

ROLLED SOUFFLE FLORENTINE

A filled souffle that never fails or falls, this dramatic and beautiful entree can even be reheated if necessary.

Souffle:
- 1 can (10 3/4 ounces) condensed cream of chicken soup
- 6 eggs, separated

Filling:
- 2 cups very finely chopped raw spinach (about 1/2 package)
- 4 ounces cream cheese, softened
- 1/2 teaspoon onion salt

Oil a jelly-roll pan (15x10x1"); line with aluminum foil, extending about 3 inches beyond pan on each end (smooth foil). Oil and lightly flour bottom and sides of foil. <u>To make souffle:</u> In saucepan, heat soup; stir occasionally. Remove from heat; cool slightly. With an electric mixer, beat egg yolks until thick and lemon-colored (about 5 minutes); stir into soup. In large bowl, using clean beaters, beat egg whites until stiff but not dry; gradually fold soup mixture into egg whites. Spread evenly in jelly-roll pan. Bake at 350°F. for 20 minutes or until done. Turn out onto waxed paper-lined large cookie sheet; gently remove foil. Meanwhile, <u>to make filling:</u> Combine spinach, cheese, and onion salt. Spread mixture evenly to within 1-inch of edges. With aid of waxed paper, roll up jelly-roll fashion starting at narrow end. Bake 5 minutes more.

Sauce:
1 teaspoon basil leaves, crushed	2 tablespoons grated Parmesan cheese
2 tablespoons butter or margarine	2 tablespoons water
1 can (10 3/4 ounces) condensed tomato soup	1 tablespoon wine vinegar
	Generous dash pepper

<u>To make sauce:</u> In saucepan, cook basil in butter; add remaining ingredients. Heat; stir occasionally. Serve over souffle. Makes 6 servings.

KAUAI CHICKEN

Chicken and spinach are combined with spices and fruit of the Pacific for a dinner evoking memories of the islands.

2 whole chicken breasts, split, skinned, boned, and cut in strips (1 pound boneless)
1/4 teaspoon ground ginger
2 tablespoons salad oil
1 can (10 3/4 ounces) condensed cream of shrimp soup

1 cup bamboo shoots
1 tablespoon soy sauce
6 cups fresh spinach torn in bite-size pieces (about 6 ounces)
1/2 cup orange sections
1/2 cup toasted whole almonds or cashews

In skillet, cook chicken with ginger in hot oil until white (about 5 minutes), stirring constantly. Add soup, bamboo shoots, and soy. Cover; cook over low heat 3 minutes. Add spinach; cook 3 minutes more or until done. Stir in oranges and almonds. Serve with additional soy. Makes about 5 cups.

POISSON ET CHAMPIGNONS

Stuffed flounder fillets are handsomely embellished with a smooth mushroom-wine sauce.

2 packages (10 ounces each) frozen asparagus spears, cooked and drained
8 fillets of flounder (about 2 pounds)
1 can (10 3/4 ounces) condensed cream of mushroom soup

1/4 cup chablis or other dry white wine
2 tablespoons grated Parmesan cheese

Divide asparagus among fillets; roll up. Secure with toothpicks. Arrange in 3-quart shallow baking dish (13x9x2"). Bake at 350°F. for 20 minutes. Meanwhile, combine remaining ingredients; pour over fish, stirring into liquid around fish. Bake 15 minutes more or until done. Stir sauce before serving. Makes 8 servings.

CRAB AND ARTICHOKE BAKE

Seafood flavored subtly with dry white wine and Cheddar cheese soup becomes elegant dining in a brief 20 minutes.

1 can (11 ounces) condensed Cheddar cheese soup
1/3 cup chablis or other dry white wine
1 teaspoon Dijon mustard
Generous dash hot pepper sauce

1 1/2 cups cooked Alaskan King crab meat or cut-up shrimp
1 package (9 ounces) frozen artichoke hearts, cooked and drained
Buttered croutons

In 1 1/2-quart shallow baking dish (10x6x2"), combine soup, wine, mustard, and hot pepper sauce; add crab meat and artichoke hearts. Bake at 400°F. for 15 minutes or until hot; stir. Top with croutons; bake 5 minutes more. Makes about 3 cups.

TAHITIAN CHICKEN

South Pacific flavors and textures enhance the chicken and create a festive dish.

2 pounds chicken parts
2 tablespoons shortening
2 cups celery diagonally
   sliced in 1-inch pieces
1/2 cup chopped onion
1/2 teaspoon ground ginger

1 can (10 3/4 ounces) condensed
   cream of chicken soup
1 can (about 11 ounces)
   mandarin orange segments,
   drained
Toasted shredded coconut

In skillet, brown chicken in shortening; pour off fat. Add remaining ingredients except oranges and coconut. Cover; cook over low heat 45 minutes or until done. Stir occasionally. Add oranges; heat. Garnish with coconut. Makes 4 servings.

COQ AU VIN

So popular a dish that we think of it as American. Yet chicken in wine came to us from the French. A bow to the chefs who released a few of their secrets.

4 slices bacon
2 pounds chicken parts
1 can (10 3/4 ounces) condensed
   chicken broth
1/2 cup chablis or other dry
   white wine
1 can (about 4 ounces) sliced
   mushrooms, drained

1/2 cup sliced onion
1 medium bay leaf
1 large clove garlic, minced
1/4 teaspoon thyme leaves,
   crushed
1/2 cup water
3 tablespoons flour

In skillet, cook bacon until crisp; remove. Pour off all but 2 tablespoons drippings. Brown chicken in drippings; pour off fat. Add soup, wine, mushrooms, onion, bay leaf, garlic, and thyme. Cover; cook over low heat 45 minutes or until done. Stir occasionally. Remove bay leaf. Gradually blend water into flour until smooth; slowly stir into sauce. Cook, stirring until thickened. Garnish with parsley and bacon. Makes 4 servings.

CHICKEN IN PLUM SAUCE

A "plum" good sauce to brush over chicken for a change of pace.

1 can (about 16 ounces) whole
   pitted purple plums, drained
1 can (10 3/4 ounces) condensed
   chicken broth
2 tablespoons cornstarch

2 tablespoons honey
2 tablespoons orange juice
   concentrate
1 teaspoon Worcestershire
3 pounds chicken parts

To make sauce, force plums through sieve. In saucepan, combine sieved plums and remaining ingredients except chicken. Cook, stirring until thickened. Arrange chicken skin-side down in shallow baking pan (13x9x2"). Brush with sauce. Bake at 400°F. for 1 hour or until done, turning chicken and brushing with sauce every 20 minutes. Spoon off fat. Makes 4 to 6 servings.

GOLDEN CHICKEN WITH POTATOES

Sweet potatoes and chicken are as southern as the saying, "Y'all come back now". And who wouldn't remember one of their very own dishes?

2 pounds chicken parts
2 tablespoons shortening
1 can (10 3/4 ounces) condensed golden mushroom soup
2 medium sweet potatoes (about 1 pound), cut in 1/2-inch slices

1/4 cup water
1/2 teaspoon onion salt
1/8 teaspoon ground nutmeg
1/2 cup seedless red grapes cut in half

In skillet, brown chicken in shortening; pour off fat. Stir in remaining ingredients except grapes. Cover; cook over low heat 45 minutes or until done. Stir occasionally. Add grapes; heat. Makes 4 servings.

LEMON HERBED CHICKEN

Because its roots grow in serpentine fashion, tarragon is often referred to as little dragon. In this recipe tarragon flavors a chicken soup-lemon sauce.

2 pounds chicken parts
2 tablespoons shortening
1 can (10 3/4 ounces) condensed cream of chicken soup
2 tablespoons lemon juice

1/2 teaspoon paprika
1/2 teaspoon salt
1/8 teaspoon tarragon leaves, crushed
Dash pepper

In skillet, brown chicken in shortening; pour off fat. Add remaining ingredients. Cover; cook over low heat 45 minutes or until done. Stir occasionally. Garnish with lemon slices. Makes 4 servings.

MEXICAN CHICKEN BAKE

Lower the heat from this spicy dish by serving an avocado-orange salad on mixed greens.

2 cups coarsely crushed taco-flavored corn chips
1 can (10 3/4 ounces) condensed cream of chicken soup
1 can (10 ounces) hot enchilada sauce

3 cups cubed cooked chicken
1/2 cup finely chopped onion
1 cup shredded sharp Cheddar cheese

In buttered 2-quart shallow baking dish (12x8x2"), combine 1 cup corn chips and remaining ingredients except cheese. Bake at 375°F. for 30 minutes or until hot; stir. Top with remaining corn chips and cheese. Bake 5 minutes more or until cheese melts. Makes about 5 cups.

FESTIVE CHINESE CHICKEN

The Chinese have much more than proverbs to share. How about frozen Chinese pea pods that lend a slightly sweet, delicate touch to chicken?

2 pounds chicken parts
2 tablespoons shortening
1 can (10 3/4 ounces) condensed chicken broth
1 medium clove garlic, minced
1 tablespoon soy sauce
1/2 teaspoon ground ginger
4 medium carrots (about 1/2 pound), cut diagonally in very thin slices

1 package (about 6 ounces) frozen pea pods
1/4 cup water
2 tablespoons cornstarch
Cooked rice

In skillet, brown chicken in shortening; pour off fat. Stir in broth, garlic, soy, and ginger. Cover; cook over low heat 35 minutes. Add carrots; cook 10 minutes more or until done. Stir occasionally. Add pea pods. Gradually blend water into cornstarch until smooth; slowly stir into sauce. Cook, stirring until thickened. Serve with rice and additional soy. Makes 4 servings.

RICE STUFFED ROCK CORNISH HENS

Carrots and raisins, so often associated with salad, reach out to lend flavor to a rice stuffing moistened with chicken broth.

2 Rock Cornish hens (about 1 1/2 pounds each)
Salt
Pepper
3 tablespoons butter or margarine, melted
1 can (10 3/4 ounces) condensed chicken broth
1/4 cup water

1/2 cup raw regular rice
1/3 cup shredded carrots
1/4 cup raisins
2 tablespoons chopped parsley
1/2 teaspoon onion powder
1/2 teaspoon salt
1 can (10 1/2 ounces) chicken gravy

Season cavity of hens with salt and pepper; chop giblets. To make stuffing, in saucepan, brown giblets in 1 tablespoon butter. Add broth, water, rice, carrots, raisins, parsley, onion powder, and 1/2 teaspoon salt. Bring to boil; reduce heat. Cover; simmer 30 minutes or until done. Stir occasionally. Fill cavity of hens loosely with stuffing. Truss; place breast-side up on rack in shallow roasting pan. Brush with remaining butter. Roast at 400°F. for 1 hour 15 minutes. Remove hens to serving platter; keep warm. On top of range, in roasting pan, stir gravy into drippings. Heat, stirring to loosen browned bits. Serve with hens and stuffing. Makes 4 servings.

SUNSHINE CHICKEN

Nutmeg and mace are often referred to as sister spices since they come from the same tropical peachlike fruit. Mace is more pungent—so good with orange and chicken.

2 pounds chicken parts	1/8 teaspoon ground mace
2 tablespoons shortening	1/8 teaspoon grated orange rind
1 can (10 3/4 ounces) condensed chicken broth	4 orange slices
	2 tablespoons cornstarch
3/4 cup orange juice	2 tablespoons water
2 teaspoons brown sugar	Cooked rice

In skillet, brown chicken in shortening; pour off fat. Stir in soup, juice, sugar, and mace. Cover; cook over low heat 40 minutes. Add oranges and rind; cook 5 minutes more or until done. Mix cornstarch and water until smooth; stir into sauce. Cook, stirring until thickened. Serve with rice. Makes 4 servings.

CHICKEN BREASTS MARSALA

A wide variety of wines are successfully used in cooking. Marsala is the choice to add distinction in this dish.

3 whole chicken breasts, split (about 3 pounds)	1/3 cup water
	2 tablespoons Marsala
2 tablespoons butter or margarine	1 medium clove garlic, minced
	1/2 teaspoon paprika
1 can (10 3/4 ounces) condensed cream of mushroom soup	Dash pepper

In skillet, slowly cook chicken in butter until done (about 30 minutes). Remove chicken to heated platter. Stir remaining ingredients into drippings. Heat; stir occasionally. Serve over chicken. Makes 6 servings.

CHICKEN ASPARAGUS RAMEKINS

Creativity in the kitchen relaxes today's busy people. These delicious ramekins with a mushroom soup base are a delight to make after a hectic day, yet take very little time or effort to prepare.

1 can (10 3/4 ounces) condensed cream of mushroom soup	1 can (5 ounces) chunk white chicken or 1 can (about 7 ounces) tuna, drained and flaked
1/4 cup milk	
1 tablespoon sherry	1/2 cup bread cubes
1 package (10 ounces) frozen cut asparagus, cooked and drained	2 tablespoons butter or margarine, melted

Blend soup, milk, and sherry. Add asparagus and chicken. Spoon into 3 individual baking dishes. Toss bread cubes with butter; place on chicken mixture. Bake at 400°F. for 15 minutes or until hot. Makes 3 servings.

CHICKEN IN CHEDDAR SAUCE

A colorful collection of vegetables adds a delicate touch of garden flavors to cheesy chicken.

3 pounds chicken parts
3 tablespoons shortening
2 cans (11 ounces each) condensed Cheddar cheese soup
1 can (about 16 ounces) tomatoes, drained and chopped
1 cup sliced onion
1 teaspoon dried dill weed, crushed
1 teaspoon salt
1 package (9 ounces) frozen cut green beans
1 package (10 ounces) frozen cauliflower
1/4 cup water
1 to 2 tablespoons flour
Cooked noodles

In large heavy pan, brown chicken in shortening; pour off fat. Add soup, tomatoes, onion, and seasonings. Cover; cook over low heat 25 minutes. Add beans and cauliflower; cook 20 minutes more or until done. Stir occasionally. Remove chicken and vegetables to serving dish; keep warm. Gradually blend water into flour until smooth; slowly stir into sauce. Cook, stirring until thickened. Serve with chicken mixture and noodles. Makes 6 servings.

TURKEY WITH APPLE AND YAMS

Turkey drumsticks, roasted spiced yams and apple can add to festivities at holidays or any time.

4 turkey drumsticks (about 4 pounds)
1/2 cup water
1 can (11 ounces) condensed Cheddar cheese soup
1/2 cup chopped onion
1 teaspoon salt
1/4 teaspoon ground allspice
Generous dash ground cloves
Generous dash ground nutmeg
1 1/2 cups finely chopped apples
4 medium sweet potatoes or yams (about 1 pound), cut in half
1/2 cup water
1/4 cup flour

In roasting pan (15 1/2x10 1/2x2 1/4"), arrange drumsticks; pour in water. Cover. Roast at 350°F. for 1 hour; turn drumsticks. Meanwhile, combine soup, onion, seasonings, and apples. Stir into drippings. Add potatoes. Cover; roast 1 hour more or until done. Meanwhile, gradually stir water into flour until smooth. Remove turkey and potatoes to platter; keep warm. On top of range, in roasting pan, gradually stir flour mixture into sauce. Cook, stirring until thickened. Serve with turkey and potatoes. Makes 8 servings.

SPRING GARDEN CHICKEN

Spring vegetables, freshly picked from the garden offer cooked chicken a new look and flavor as they simmer in cream of chicken soup. Patty shells spell convenience.

2 green onions, sliced
1 teaspoon dried dill weed, crushed
2 tablespoons butter or margarine
1 can (10 3/4 ounces) condensed cream of chicken soup

1/2 cup milk
1 1/2 cups cubed cooked chicken
1 large cucumber, quartered and sliced (about 2 cups)
1/2 cup sliced radishes
1/2 teaspoon salt
Patty shells

In saucepan, cook onions with dill in butter until tender. Add remaining ingredients except patty shells. Heat; stir occasionally. Serve over patty shells. Makes about 4 cups.

CURRIED SHRIMP

Curried shrimp for dinner? Remember the side dishes of complementary foods . . . chutney, chopped apple and green pepper to sprinkle over the shrimp.

1/2 cup diagonally sliced celery
1/2 cup sliced onion
1 small clove garlic, minced
1 tablespoon curry powder
1/8 teaspoon ground ginger
2 tablespoons butter or margarine
1 can (10 3/4 ounces) condensed chicken broth

1 tablespoon honey
1 pound frozen cleaned raw shrimp
1/2 to 2/3 cup water
1/4 to 1/3 cup flour
Cooked rice
Chopped apple, chutney, peanuts, and green pepper

In saucepan, cook celery and onion with garlic, curry, and ginger in butter until tender. Add broth and honey. Bring to boil; add shrimp. Reduce heat; simmer 5 minutes or until done. Stir occasionally. Gradually blend water into flour until smooth; slowly stir into broth mixture. Cook, stirring until thickened. Serve over rice with a variety of remaining ingredients. Makes about 3 1/2 cups.

LANCASTER CHICKEN AND VEGETABLES

This quick and easy use of canned chicken and leftovers is reminiscent of the venerable Pennsylvania Dutch cuisine.

2 slices bacon
1 can (10 3/4 ounces) condensed cream of mushroom soup
1/2 cup shredded sharp Cheddar cheese
1 tablespoon vinegar
1 teaspoon sugar
1 medium clove garlic, minced
1 cup sliced cooked carrots
1 1/2 cups cubed cooked potatoes
1 cup diced fresh tomatoes
1 can (5 ounces) chunk white chicken
1/4 cup chopped parsley

In skillet, cook bacon until crisp; remove and crumble. Stir in soup, cheese, vinegar, sugar, and garlic. Heat until cheese melts; stir occasionally. Add bacon and remaining ingredients; heat. Makes about 4 cups.

SHRIMP NEWBURG

Generously fill patty shells with this interesting variation on a classic newburg. The center of attraction for any meal.

1 cup sliced fresh mushrooms (about 1/4 pound)
1/4 cup diced green pepper
2 tablespoons butter or margarine
2 cans (11 ounces each) condensed Cheddar cheese soup
2 tablespoons tomato paste
1/3 cup dry sherry
1/8 teaspoon hot pepper sauce
2 pounds medium shrimp (31 to 35/pound), cooked, shelled, and deveined
2 tablespoons pimiento strips
2 eggs, well beaten
1/3 cup heavy cream
Patty shells

In large saucepan, brown mushrooms and cook green pepper in butter until tender. Blend in soup, tomato paste, sherry, and hot pepper sauce. Add shrimp and pimiento. Heat; stir occasionally. Meanwhile, combine eggs and cream. Blend about 1 cup hot soup mixture into egg mixture; gradually blend into remaining soup mixture. Cook over low heat, stirring until just thickened. Serve over patty shells. Makes about 6 cups.

POACHED FISH

The poaching liquid becomes the base for the delicate sauce which enhances the flavor of the white fish itself.

1 can (10 3/4 ounces) condensed chicken broth
1/4 cup chopped green onions
2 tablespoons dry vermouth
Dash pepper

2 pounds fillets of white fish
2 tablespoons cornstarch
2 tablespoons water
1 egg yolk, slightly beaten

In skillet, combine broth, onions, vermouth, and pepper; add fish. Cover; cook over low heat 10 minutes or until done. Remove fish to serving platter; keep warm. Meanwhile, combine cornstarch, water, and egg yolk. Gradually blend into broth mixture. Cook, stirring until thickened. Serve over fish. Makes 6 servings.

TEMPURA

A light shrimp-flavored batter coats chicken and vegetables for quick cooking in a wok. The piquant sauces for tempura are a must and can be made in minutes.

1 can (10 3/4 ounces) condensed cream of shrimp soup
1 cup flour
1 egg, slightly beaten
1/2 teaspoon salt
1 small eggplant (about 3/4 pound), peeled and cubed

3 chicken breasts, split, skinned, and boned (1 1/2 pounds boneless)
1 medium Bermuda onion, sliced
1 medium green pepper, cut in 1-inch squares
Salad oil

In bowl, combine soup, flour, egg, and salt. Chill 30 minutes or until ready to use. Meanwhile, salt eggplant; let stand 30 minutes. Pat dry. Cut chicken into bite-size pieces. Dip chicken and vegetables into soup batter to coat lightly. Half-fill wok or large saucepan with oil; preheat to 375°F. Cook chicken (about 5 minutes) and vegetables (about 3 minutes), a few pieces at a time, until lightly browned. Drain; keep warm. Serve with dipping sauces. Makes 6 servings.

Sherry Soy Sauce
1 cup condensed beef broth
1/4 cup dry sherry
1/4 cup soy sauce

Mustard Sauce
1/4 cup dry mustard
1/4 cup water

In small saucepan, combine ingredients. Heat; stir occasionally. Makes about 1 1/2 cups.

In small dish (about 1/2 cup size) combine mustard and water. Makes about 1/2 cup.

SHRIMP STUFFED ARTICHOKES

The aristocratic artichoke goes back to the days of Roman banquets. Their delicate taste and artistic presentation make this a dish worthy of many compliments.

1/2 cup chopped celery
1 medium clove garlic, minced
2 tablespoons butter or margarine
1 can (10 3/4 ounces) condensed cream of shrimp soup
1/2 cup light cream
1 tablespoon lemon juice
Generous dash crushed tarragon leaves

1 pound medium shrimp (31 to 35/pound), cooked and drained
4 large whole artichokes, cooked
Salad oil
1/4 cup buttered bread crumbs
Shredded Monterey Jack or Cheddar cheese

In saucepan, cook celery with garlic in butter until tender. Stir in soup, light cream, lemon juice, tarragon, and shrimp. Heat; stir occasionally. Separate artichoke petals to form a cup; remove choke. Lightly oil a 2-quart shallow baking dish (12x8x2″). Arrange artichoke cups in baking dish. Fill each with shrimp mixture. Top with bread crumbs and cheese. Bake at 400°F. for 20 minutes or until hot. Makes 4 servings.

ALASKAN CRAB FONDUE

Baked fondue is the Americanized version of the classic Swiss dish. Prepared in an attractive casserole, it can be easily taken right from the oven and served at the table.

1 can (10 3/4 ounces) condensed cream of mushroom soup
1/2 cup milk
1 cup shredded Cheddar cheese
1 package (6 ounces) frozen Alaskan King crab meat, thawed and drained

2 cups bread cubes
1/2 teaspoon dry mustard
1/2 teaspoon Worcestershire
Dash pepper
4 eggs, separated

In saucepan, combine soup, milk, and cheese; heat until cheese melts. Blend in crab, bread cubes, mustard, Worcestershire, and pepper. Beat egg yolks until thick and lemon-colored. Gradually stir in crab mixture. Beat egg whites until stiff but not dry; fold in soup mixture. Pour into 1 1/2-quart casserole. Bake at 325°F. for 1 hour or until knife inserted in center comes out clean. Makes 4 servings.

SANPAN TURKEY

Canned Chinese vegetables usually contain bean sprouts, bamboo shoots and others in smaller amounts and colors. When mixed with the green broccoli they appeal to the taste.

1 turkey breast (about
    4 pounds)
2 tablespoons shortening
1 can (10 3/4 ounces) condensed
    golden mushroom soup
2 tablespoons dry sherry
1 tablespoon soy sauce

1 large clove garlic, minced
1/8 teaspoon ground ginger
1 package (10 ounces) frozen
    broccoli spears, partially thawed
    and cut in 1-inch pieces
1 can (16 ounces) Chinese
    vegetables, drained

In large heavy pan, brown turkey in shortening; pour off fat. Arrange turkey meat-side down. Add soup, sherry, soy, garlic, and ginger. Cover; cook over low heat 1 hour. Turn turkey meat-side up. Add broccoli and Chinese vegetables; cook 30 minutes more or until done. Stir occasionally. Remove turkey and vegetables to serving platter; keep warm. Thicken sauce if desired. Makes 6 servings.

LAYERED CHEESE AND NOODLE BAKE

Cheese and noodles come to the rescue as ingredients for many dishes. This variation of lasagna with a blend of cheese flavors is easily prepared.

1 cup chopped onion
2 teaspoons oregano leaves,
    crushed
2 tablespoons butter or
    margarine
2 cans (10 3/4 ounces each)
    condensed tomato soup
1/2 cup water
1/4 teaspoon salt
Generous dash pepper

4 cups cooked wide noodles
1 package (10 ounces) frozen
    chopped spinach, cooked and
    well drained
1 pound small curd creamed style
    cottage cheese (about 2 cups)
4 slices (about 4 ounces) Provolone
    cheese, quartered
Grated Parmesan cheese

In large saucepan, cook onion with oregano in butter until tender. Add soup, water, salt, pepper, and noodles. Spoon 1/3 noodle mixture into 3-quart casserole; top with 1/2 spinach and 1/2 cottage cheese. Arrange 2 slices Provolone on cottage cheese. Top with 1/3 noodle mixture, remaining spinach, and remaining cottage cheese. Sprinkle with Parmesan cheese. Arrange remaining noodle mixture around edge of casserole; top with remaining Provolone cheese. Bake at 400°F. for 35 minutes. Makes 8 servings.

DEVILED CRAB

Dry mustard and Worcestershire sauce "devil" these individual portions of baked crab in cheese soup.

1 cup sliced fresh mushrooms
(about 1/4 pound)
1/2 cup chopped onion
1/4 cup chopped green pepper
1/4 teaspoon dry mustard
2 tablespoons butter or
margarine

1 can (11 ounces) condensed
Cheddar cheese soup
1 tablespoon Worcestershire
2 packages (6 ounces each) frozen
Alaskan King crab meat, thawed
and drained
1/4 cup buttered bread crumbs

In saucepan, brown mushrooms and cook onion and green pepper with mustard in butter until tender. Stir in soup, Worcestershire, and crab. Divide among 4 individual baking dishes; sprinkle with bread crumbs. Bake at 400°F. for 15 minutes or until hot. Makes 4 servings.

OMELETTE POULET

Want something special at a moment's notice? These commonly used ingredients can be kept on hand and turned into an exciting recipe for the omelet chef in your house.

1/2 cup sliced green onions
1/4 cup chopped celery
5 tablespoons butter or
margarine
1 can (5 ounces) chunk white
chicken

1 can (10 3/4 ounces) condensed
golden mushroom soup
1/2 cup Italian seasoned croutons
8 large eggs

To make filling, in saucepan, cook 1/4 cup onions and celery in 2 tablespoons butter until tender. Stir in 1/2 can chicken, 1/4 cup soup, and croutons. Heat, stirring; set aside. To make omelet, beat eggs and 1/4 cup soup. In omelet pan or small skillet, melt 1 tablespoon butter; pour in about 1/2 cup egg mixture. Cook slowly; as undersurface becomes set, lift slightly to allow uncooked egg to flow underneath and cook. Place 1/4 cup chicken mixture on omelet; fold over. Keep warm. Repeat making 3 more omelets. Meanwhile, to make sauce, in saucepan, cook remaining onions in 2 tablespoons butter until tender. Stir in remaining soup and chicken. Heat; stir occasionally. Serve over omelets. Makes 4 servings.

JAMBALAYA

Jambalaya, the champion of creole dishes, is made easy in this quick version which uses condensed chicken broth.

1 cup cubed cooked ham
1 medium clove garlic, minced
2 tablespoons butter or margarine
1 can (10 3/4 ounces) condensed
  chicken broth
1 can (about 16 ounces)
  tomatoes, cut up
1/2 cup sliced onion

1/2 cup chopped green pepper
2 tablespoons Worcestershire
1/2 teaspoon thyme leaves,
  crushed
Generous dash cayenne pepper
1 pound medium shrimp (31 to
  35/pound), shelled and deveined
1 cup raw regular rice

In skillet, brown ham with garlic in butter. Stir in remaining ingredients except shrimp and rice. Bring to boil; add shrimp and rice. Reduce heat; cover. Simmer 20 minutes or until done. Stir occasionally. Makes about 6 1/2 cups.

NAPOLI MOLD

Pasta is made dramatic in this lasagna noodle-lined ring mold. The delicate filling is lightly seasoned in the northern Italian style.

11 lasagna noodles, cooked,
  rinsed, and drained
Butter or margarine, melted
1 can (10 3/4 ounces) condensed
  cream of celery soup
4 eggs, slightly beaten

1/4 cup milk
3 cups cooked fine noodles
1 cup ricotta cheese
3/4 cup grated Parmesan cheese
1/2 cup chopped parsley
1 teaspoon basil leaves, crushed

Lay lasagna noodles between towels; pat dry. Line a 6 1/2-cup well-buttered ring mold with lasagna noodles as follows: Overlap noodles letting ends hang over sides of mold 2 inches (trim ends if necessary). Brush noodles with melted butter. To make filling, in bowl, combine soup, eggs, and milk. Stir in fine noodles, cheeses, parsley, and basil. Spoon into noodle-lined mold; fold noodle ends over top. Brush with additional butter. Bake at 350°F. for 45 minutes; let stand 10 minutes before serving. To unmold, carefully run spatula around insides of mold. Invert on large plate; invert again onto serving platter. Serve with stewed tomatoes. Makes 8 servings.

SALMON STEAKS WITH DILL SAUCE

Dill is a natural complement for cucumbers and salmon. Here all three are combined to create a subtle, distinctive taste.

1 can (10 3/4 ounces) condensed chicken broth
2 tablespoons lemon juice
1/2 cup chopped cucumber
1/3 cup chopped onion
1 teaspoon dried dill weed, crushed

4 fresh salmon steaks (about 2 pounds)
2 tablespoons light cream
2 tablespoons flour

In skillet, combine broth, lemon juice, cucumber, onion, and dill; add salmon. Cover; cook over low heat 10 minutes or until done. Remove salmon to platter; keep warm. Meanwhile, gradually blend cream into flour until smooth; slowly stir into sauce. Cook, stirring until thickened. Garnish with parsley and lemon wedges. Makes 4 servings.

HAM QUICHE

A colorful polka dot quiche that brings a festive flair to your table.

1 can (10 3/4 ounces) condensed cream of chicken soup
4 eggs, slightly beaten
1/2 cup light cream
4 teaspoons flour
1 cup shredded sharp Cheddar cheese
1/4 cup finely chopped cooked ham

2 tablespoons finely chopped celery
2 tablespoons finely chopped onion
2 tablespoons finely chopped green pepper
2 tablespoons finely chopped pimiento
9-inch baked pie shell

In bowl, combine soup, eggs, and cream. Toss flour with remaining ingredients except pie shell; sprinkle over bottom of pie shell. Pour egg mixture over vegetable mixture. Bake at 350°F. for 45 minutes or until knife inserted in center comes out clean.* Let stand 15 minutes before serving. Makes 4 to 6 servings.

*If necessary during baking, cover edges of pie shell with aluminum foil to prevent overbrowning.

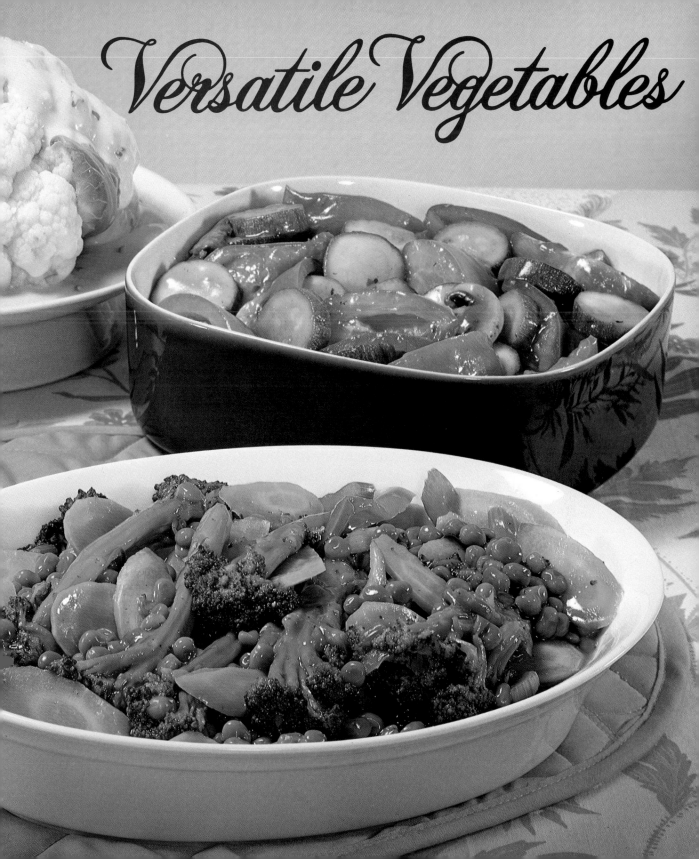

Versatile Vegetables

Versatile Vegetables

Sometimes we eat the stems, sometimes the fruits, other times the flowers, roots, seeds or leaves. What are they? Vegetables, of course.

Tomatoes, cucumbers and squash are fruits, while cauliflower and broccoli are flowers. Peas, beans and corn are seeds and spinach, lettuce and cabbage are leaves. It's interesting to think of vegetables in this way. The history of these gifts of the garden is fascinating too.

Early non-agricultural man survived by eating what nature provided, often the wild ancestors of plants that we use today. Gradually, he began to domesticate some of these. Archeological evidence shows that by 2000 B.C. peoples of Africa, Asia and Europe were growing onions, leeks, cucumbers, cabbage, broad beans, soy beans and turnips.

The Greeks and Romans prized vegetables and cultivated a great number. Long growing seasons and mild Mediterranean climate were factors which contributed to their interest and enjoyment of vegetables.

The Greeks enjoyed wild asparagus, dried peas, lettuce, lentils and cabbage. The Romans ate cucumbers, radishes, cauliflower and leeks. The ancient "favorite" list goes on — broccoli, eggplant, turnips, parsnips and, one of the oldest of vegetables, the chick pea.

Historically, vegetables have been used in some rather unusual ways. Parsley was not only a favorite garnish and flavoring, but it also was used in festive garlands for the head of victorious athletes and warriors, and in bouquets to decorate dining halls. Carrots and celery were grown strictly for medicinal purposes. Through the years, folklore developed around the virtues of vegetables. The lowly leek even became the national symbol for Welshmen commemorating their victory over the Saxons.

Global exploration has always promoted the sharing of foodstuffs between cultures. Vegetables were "traded" extensively. Tomatoes, potatoes, corn, squash, pumpkins, chili peppers and green beans were all gifts from the New World to the Old.

Corn was a very important vegetable for early settlers in this country. At Plymouth Colony, Indians showed them how to plant, harvest and cook this "new" food.

The golden pumpkin was also used extensively. A Plymouth song gives us an indication of the role it played in the colonists' diet:

> "We have pumpkins at morning,
> pumpkins at noon
> If it were not for pumpkins
> We should be undoon."

In the United States, commercial ice production and the development of a rail system in the mid 1800's led to the distribution of vegetables beyond their immediate growing locale. Gradually, as the vast rail system spread, opening up the West, and as the California farm valleys were irrigated, fresh vegetables became more available. The possibility of having fresh produce year-round was no longer just a dream.

Canned vegetables were introduced to the troops during the Civil War and the technology for freezing fresh produce was developed in the 20th century. Now, modern technologies in transportation and processing supply Americans with a daily cornucopia of vegetables.

The versatility of vegetables is overwhelming!

Consider what they offer just in flavor and texture. They can be sweet or sour, crisp or tender, bland or tangy. They can be served hot or cold. They also offer color — every hue of the rainbow and can be mixed with a myriad of other foods for even greater variety.

This chapter contains exciting ideas and interesting ways to prepare vegetables. For color alone, the Confetti Rice in the preceding photograph illustrates how crisp and bright the simple combination of rice, peas and pimiento can be.

Complementing the gentle flavor of the cauliflower is a velvety cream sauce made with Cheddar cheese soup and sour cream. Green onion and lemon juice bring a piquant touch.

The dramatic Vegetable Melange in the foreground is an oriental style celebration of carrots and broccoli simmered in chicken broth and laced with soy and ginger seasonings.

Vegetables A La Grecque is truly a festive sight. Its wedges of red tomatoes coupled with zucchini slices, mushrooms and green pepper are cooked in condensed beef broth and a few seasonings.

Another dish with Mediterranean sparkle is Amalfi Green Beans. In it Italian green beans and fresh mushrooms are touched with flavors of basil and onion and served with crisp bacon morsels.

These are just the beginning of wonders to be explored with vegetables. The following pages are filled with interesting suggestions for marinating, baking, stir-frying or preparing them with unusual sauces. Truly, the only limitation to the versatility of the vegetable is the imagination of the cook.

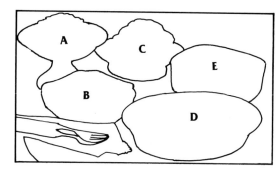

A CONFETTI RICE
B AMALFI GREEN BEANS
C CAULIFLOWER AU GRATIN
D VEGETABLE MELANGE
E VEGETABLES A LA GRECQUE

VEGETABLE MELANGE

Four readily available vegetables simmer in a favorite Chinese cooking liquid—condensed chicken broth. Ginger and soy sauce enhance the broth.

1 can (10 3/4 ounces) condensed
    chicken broth
2 tablespoons cornstarch
1 tablespoon soy sauce
1/4 teaspoon ground ginger
2 packages (10 ounces each)
    frozen broccoli spears

1 package (10 ounces) frozen peas
1/2 cup carrots thinly sliced
    diagonally
1/2 cup diagonally sliced celery

In skillet, combine broth, cornstarch, soy, and ginger; add vegetables. Bring to boil, stirring. Reduce heat. Cover; simmer 10 minutes or until done. Stir occasionally. Serve with additional soy. Makes about 5 1/2 cups.

BROCCOLI AND ONION ALMONDINE

Dip into these curried vegetables with a large spoon. Out come creamy onions and broccoli with a sprinkling of toasted almonds. Yes, a second serving is available.

1 can (10 3/4 ounces) condensed
    cream of mushroom soup
1/4 cup milk
1/2 teaspoon curry powder
1 pound (about 16) small
    whole white onions, cooked
    and drained

1 package (10 ounces) frozen
    chopped broccoli, cooked
    and drained
Toasted slivered almonds

In saucepan, combine soup, milk, and curry; add onions and broccoli. Heat a few minutes to blend flavors. Stir occasionally. Garnish with almonds. Makes about 4 cups.

YAMS IN A CASSEROLE

Fluffy yams, mashed with consomme, brown sugar and spice, are spooned into a casserole and dotted with pecans. Serve with baked ham or poultry.

4 cans (about 16 ounces each)
    yams or sweet potatoes, drained
1 can (10 1/2 ounces)
    condensed consomme

1/4 cup brown sugar
1/4 teaspoon ground nutmeg
1/4 teaspoon salt
1/2 cup pecan halves

Mash potatoes, gradually adding consomme, brown sugar, nutmeg, and salt. Continue beating until light and fluffy. Spoon into 2-quart casserole. Bake at 400°F. for 40 minutes or until hot. Garnish with pecans. Makes about 6 cups.

ITALIAN QUICHE

This cheese and egg pie with zucchini, onion and Italian spices is very exciting in flavor. While it makes 6 servings, three hungry men might devour it all.

9-inch unbaked pie shell
3 slices bacon
1/4 cup finely chopped onion
1/4 teaspoon basil leaves,
    crushed
1/4 teaspoon oregano leaves,
    crushed
1 small clove garlic, minced

1 can (11 ounces) condensed
    Cheddar cheese soup
2 cups mashed cooked zucchini
    (about 3 medium)
3 eggs, slightly beaten
1/3 cup grated Parmesan cheese
1 tablespoon flour
Paprika

Partially bake pie shell at 350°F. for 10 minutes. Meanwhile, in skillet, cook bacon until crisp; remove and crumble. Cook onion with basil, oregano, and garlic in drippings until tender. Stir in remaining ingredients. Pour into pie shell; sprinkle with paprika. Bake at 350°F. for 1 hour or until knife inserted in center comes out clean. Makes 6 servings.

CORN RELISH

Pile the relish bowl high with this sweet yet spicy corn mixture. Once around the table will hardly be enough since two or three servings may disappear fast.

1 can (11 ounces) condensed
    tomato bisque soup
2 cups cooked fresh sweet corn
    cut from the cob (about
    6 medium ears)
1/2 cup sliced green onions

1/2 cup chopped green pepper
1 medium clove garlic, minced
2 tablespoons lemon juice
1 tablespoon sugar
1/4 teaspoon dry mustard
1/8 teaspoon ground turmeric

In bowl, combine ingredients; chill. Makes about 3 1/2 cups.

SPINACH SOUFFLE

Serve this souffle with sliced cold ham. Its ingredients are most complementary to ham.

1 can (10 3/4 ounces) condensed
    cream of chicken soup
1 cup shredded sharp Cheddar
    cheese
1/8 teaspoon ground nutmeg

6 eggs, separated
1 package (10 ounces) frozen
    chopped spinach, cooked
    and well drained

In saucepan, combine soup, cheese, and nutmeg; heat slowly until cheese melts. Stir occasionally. Remove from heat. Beat egg yolks until thick and lemon-colored; gradually stir into soup mixture. Add spinach. In large bowl, using a clean beater, beat egg whites until stiff; fold in soup mixture. Pour into ungreased 2-quart casserole. Bake at 300°F. for 1 hour 15 minutes. Serve immediately. Makes 4 servings.

PENNSYLVANIA DUTCH POTATO BAKE

This sweet and sour dressing is typical of "Dutch" cooking. Pour it over sliced cooked potatoes in a casserole. Bake and garnish with reserved bacon.

6 slices bacon	2 tablespoons diced pimiento
1 can (10 3/4 ounces) condensed chicken broth	1/4 cup diagonally sliced green onions
2 tablespoons flour	1/2 teaspoon celery salt
1/4 cup vinegar	1/4 teaspoon hot pepper sauce
2 tablespoons brown sugar	6 cups sliced cooked potatoes

In skillet, cook bacon until crisp; remove. Pour off all but 1/4 cup drippings. Gradually blend broth into flour until smooth; slowly stir into drippings. Add remaining ingredients except potatoes. Cook, stirring until thickened. In 1 1/2-quart shallow baking dish (10x6x2"), arrange potatoes; pour broth mixture over potatoes. Cover; bake at 400°F. for 30 minutes or until hot. Garnish with bacon. Makes about 6 cups.

MINTED PEAS AND MUSHROOMS

Thomas Jefferson grew many vegetables in his garden but his favorite was the pea. Most Americans have followed suit. Instead of serving them plain try this recipe.

1/2 pound fresh mushrooms, cut in half (about 2 cups)	1/4 cup water
1/4 cup sliced almonds	2 tablespoons chopped pimiento
2 tablespoons butter or margarine	1/2 teaspoon dried mint leaves, crushed
1 can (10 3/4 ounces) condensed cream of celery soup	1 package (10 ounces) frozen peas, cooked and drained

In saucepan, brown mushrooms and almonds in butter. Add remaining ingredients. Heat; stir occasionally. Makes about 3 cups.

CONFETTI RICE

Pimiento and peas form the confetti in this fluffy rice simmered in chicken broth.

1/2 cup raw regular rice	1 can (10 3/4 ounces) condensed chicken broth
1/8 teaspoon rubbed sage	1 cup frozen peas
2 tablespoons butter or margarine	2 tablespoons diced pimiento

In saucepan, brown rice with sage in butter. Add broth. Bring to boil; reduce heat. Simmer 15 minutes; add peas. Simmer 10 minutes more or until done. Stir occasionally. Stir in pimiento. Makes about 3 cups.

VEGETABLE MEDLEY

French fried onions from a can perform double duty. Some go into the soup and vegetables; others stay back to be used as a garnish.

1 can (10 3/4 ounces) condensed
  creamy chicken mushroom soup
1/2 cup milk
1 teaspoon soy sauce
1 package (10 ounces) frozen
  crinkle cut carrots, cooked
  and drained

1 package (10 ounces) frozen peas,
  cooked and drained
1 can (3 1/2 ounces) French fried
  onions

In saucepan, blend soup, milk, and soy; add carrots, peas, and 1/2 can onions. Heat; stir occasionally. Garnish with remaining onions. Makes about 6 1/2 cups.

HERBED STUFFED ACORN SQUASH

Stuffed acorn squash halves, with orange rind and honey added to some of the golden mushroom soup for saucing the stuffing, make a fine vegetable for pork chops.

3 medium acorn squash
Butter or margarine, melted
1/4 cup chopped celery
1/4 cup chopped onion
1/3 cup butter or margarine
1 can (10 3/4 ounces) condensed
  golden mushroom soup

2 cups packaged herb seasoned
  stuffing mix
1 cup cooked peas and carrots
1/3 cup water
3/4 teaspoon grated orange rind
2 teaspoons honey

Split squash; remove seeds and fibers. Brush inside edges with melted butter. Bake, cut side down, in shallow baking dish at 400°F. for 35 minutes. Meanwhile, in saucepan, cook celery and onion in 1/3 cup butter until tender. Add 1/2 cup soup, stuffing mix, vegetables, water, and 1/2 teaspoon orange rind. Fill squash with mixture. Bake 20 minutes more or until done. Combine remaining soup, honey, and 1/4 teaspoon orange rind. Heat; stir occasionally. Serve with squash. Makes 6 servings.

CURRIED CORN

Suitable for adult tastes is this curried corn-green vegetable medley. Ground cumin seed, a member of the carrot family, imparts its own flavor.

1/2 cup chopped celery
1/2 cup chopped onion
1/4 cup chopped green pepper
2 teaspoons curry powder
1/8 teaspoon ground cumin seed
Dash cayenne pepper

3 tablespoons butter or margarine
1 can (10 3/4 ounces) condensed
  cream of mushroom soup
1/2 cup sour cream
1 can (about 16 ounces) whole
  kernel golden corn, drained

In saucepan, cook celery, onion, and green pepper with seasonings in butter until tender. Stir in soup and sour cream; add corn. Heat; stir occasionally. Makes about 3 1/2 cups.

SWEET AND SOUR CABBAGE

The harvest is in with cabbage and apples aglow with red. Turn them into a sweet and sour dish to serve with pork or ham.

3 slices bacon
1/2 cup chopped onion
1 can (10 3/4 ounces) condensed
   chicken broth
1/4 cup red wine vinegar
2 tablespoons sugar
1/4 teaspoon salt

Generous dash pepper
1 medium bay leaf
7 cups shredded red cabbage,
   1 small head (about 1 1/2 pounds)
3 cups sliced apples, 2 medium
4 teaspoons cornstarch
2 tablespoons water

In skillet, cook bacon until crisp; remove and crumble. Cook onion in drippings until tender. Stir in chicken broth, vinegar, sugar, salt, pepper, and bay leaf. Bring to boil; add cabbage. Reduce heat; simmer 10 minutes. Arrange apples on cabbage; cook 10 minutes more or until done. Stir occasionally. Combine cornstarch and water; stir into sauce. Cook, stirring until thickened. Remove bay leaf. Garnish with bacon. Makes about 4 cups.

CORN FRITTERS

Fritters with a New England angle—the liquid being condensed clam chowder. Pass syrup while fritters are still very hot.

Salad oil
1 cup all-purpose flour
2 teaspoons baking powder
1 can (10 3/4 ounces) condensed
   New England clam chowder
2 eggs

1 cup cooked whole kernel golden
   corn
1 tablespoon salad oil
1 tablespoon finely chopped onion
1/4 teaspoon hot pepper sauce
Maple syrup

Half-fill deep fat fryer or large saucepan with oil; preheat to 400°F. In bowl, combine all ingredients except maple syrup, stirring until just blended (batter will be slightly lumpy). Drop rounded tablespoonfuls into hot oil. Fry 5 minutes or until lightly browned, turning once. Drain; keep warm. Serve with syrup. Makes 24 fritters.

BRAISED CUCUMBERS

Consider cooked cucumbers and celery for an upcoming meal. Simmer them in chicken broth with lemon juice and chervil.

4 large cucumbers (about
   2 pounds), peeled
1 can (10 3/4 ounces) condensed
   chicken broth
1 cup diagonally sliced celery

2 tablespoons diced pimiento
1 teaspoon lemon juice
1/8 teaspoon dried chervil leaves,
   crushed

Slice cucumbers in half lengthwise; remove seeds. Cut into 1-inch pieces. In saucepan, combine all ingredients. Cover; bring to boil. Simmer 5 minutes; stir occasionally. Drain.* Garnish with lemon slices. Makes about 5 cups.

*Broth: Serve broth in cups. Makes about 1 1/2 cups.

POTATO 'N BLUE CHEESE SCALLOP

Condensed mushroom soup stabilizes the cream-blue cheese mixture for baked scalloped potatoes. Serve with veal and a mixed green salad.

1 can (10 3/4 ounces) condensed cream of mushroom soup	1 teaspoon dried chopped chives
1/2 cup light cream	Generous dash pepper
1/3 cup sour cream	4 cups thinly sliced potatoes
2 tablespoons crumbled blue cheese	Paprika

Combine all ingredients except potatoes and paprika. In 1 1/2-quart casserole, arrange alternate layers of potatoes and soup mixture. Sprinkle with paprika. Cover; bake at 375°F. for 1 hour. Uncover; bake 15 minutes more or until done. Makes about 3 1/2 cups.

VEGETABLES A LA GRECQUE

Garlic, thyme and lemon juice, allowed to simmer in rich beef broth, bring out the very best flavor in this vegetable foursome.

1 small clove garlic, minced	2 teaspoons lemon juice
1/4 teaspoon thyme leaves, crushed	3 medium zucchini, cut in 1/2-inch slices (about 6 cups)
2 tablespoons butter or margarine	2 cups sliced fresh mushrooms (about 1/2 pound)
1 can (10 1/2 ounces) condensed beef broth	1 medium green pepper, cut in strips
1/4 cup water	2 large tomatoes, cut in wedges
3 tablespoons cornstarch	Grated Parmesan cheese

In large skillet, cook garlic with thyme in butter. Stir in broth, water, cornstarch, and lemon juice. Add zucchini, mushrooms, and green pepper. Bring to boil, stirring; reduce heat. Cover; simmer 15 minutes or until done. Stir occasionally. Add tomatoes; heat. Serve with cheese. Makes about 6 1/2 cups.

BLUSHING CARROT PENNIES

Sliced carrots are often referred to as pennies. Heat them in a sweet and sour tomato soup mixture. Garnish with bacon, cheese and green parsley for color contrast.

2 slices bacon	4 teaspoons vinegar
1 medium green pepper, cut in squares	1 teaspoon sugar
1 medium clove garlic, minced	3 cups sliced cooked carrots
1 can (10 3/4 ounces) condensed tomato soup	1/2 cup shredded sharp Cheddar cheese
	1/4 cup chopped parsley

In skillet, cook bacon until crisp; remove and crumble. Cook green pepper with garlic in drippings until tender. Stir in soup, vinegar, and sugar. Add bacon and remaining ingredients. Heat; stir occasionally. Makes about 3 cups.

AMBROSIA SWEET POTATOES

Lovely casserole for the winter when sweet potatoes are in abundance in the market. Oranges, coconut and pecans give a true Southern flavor.

1 can (11 ounces) condensed Cheddar cheese soup
1/4 cup packed brown sugar
1 tablespoon cornstarch
1/8 teaspoon ground cinnamon
Generous dash ground mace
4 cups thinly sliced raw sweet potatoes

1 can (about 16 ounces) sliced pineapple in pure pineapple juice, drained
2 medium oranges, peeled and sliced
1/2 cup shredded coconut
1/3 cup chopped pecans

To make sauce, combine soup, sugar, cornstarch, cinnamon, and mace. In 2-quart casserole, arrange alternate layers of potatoes, pineapple, oranges, coconut, pecans, and sauce. Cover; bake at 375°F. for 1 hour. Uncover; bake 15 minutes more or until potatoes are done. Garnish with maraschino cherries and toasted coconut. Makes 4 to 6 servings.

SUMMER VEGETABLE MEDLEY

It takes so little time to prepare this attractive vegetable dish that you'll want to repeat it again and again as part of your weekly menus.

1/4 cup chopped onion
2 tablespoons butter or margarine
1 can (10 3/4 ounces) condensed cream of mushroom soup
1/3 cup milk
1/2 cup drained cut up canned tomatoes

1 teaspoon Worcestershire
1/8 teaspoon pepper
2 cups cooked cut green beans
1 cup cooked whole kernel golden corn

In saucepan, cook onion in butter until tender. Add remaining ingredients. Heat; stir occasionally. Makes about 4 cups.

MARINATED VEGETABLE SALAD

Marinades made with tomato soup, wine vinegar, herbs and mustard bring out the best in vegetables. To this particular salad add sliced and quartered salami.

Marinade:

1 can (10 3/4 ounces) condensed
  tomato soup
1/2 cup salad oil
1/4 cup red wine vinegar
1 tablespoon sugar
1/4 teaspoon hot pepper sauce

1 large clove garlic, minced
1 1/2 teaspoons oregano leaves,
  crushed
1/4 teaspoon celery salt
1/4 teaspoon dry mustard
1/4 teaspoon pepper

Salad:

1 cup diagonally sliced
  carrots
1 cup cauliflowerets
1 medium green pepper,
  cut in squares
1 package (9 ounces) frozen
  artichoke hearts, cooked
  and drained

1 cup thickly sliced fresh
  mushrooms
1/2 cup ripe olives
4 ounces sliced salami, cut in
  quarters (about 1 cup)

In saucepan, combine marinade ingredients. Cook over low heat 10 minutes; stir occasionally. Arrange salad ingredients in 2 1/2-quart shallow baking dish (13x9x2"). Pour marinade over salad. Cover; chill 6 hours or more. Stir occasionally. With slotted spoon, arrange vegetables on platter. Makes about 7 cups.

EGGPLANT PARMA

The deep purple eggplant is especially succulent when cooked with garlic, an herb, tomato soup and two Italian cheeses.

1 medium eggplant (about
  1 pound), cubed
1 small onion, sliced
1 small clove garlic, minced
1/2 teaspoon oregano leaves,
  crushed
2 tablespoons butter or
  margarine

1 can (10 3/4 ounces) condensed
  tomato soup
1/4 cup grated Parmesan cheese
1/4 teaspoon vinegar
Generous dash pepper
Shredded mozzarella cheese

In saucepan, cook eggplant in boiling salted water 3 minutes or until done; drain. Cook onion with garlic and oregano in butter until tender. Stir in soup, eggplant, Parmesan cheese, vinegar, and pepper. Heat; stir occasionally. Garnish with mozzarella cheese. Makes about 3 cups.

AMALFI GREEN BEANS

When dried basil leaves are crushed they have a lemony-like quality. Use this herb with onion and garlic to enhance Italian green beans.

3 slices bacon, cut in half	1 can (10 3/4 ounces) condensed
2 cups sliced fresh mushrooms	tomato soup
(about 1/2 pound)	1/4 cup water
1/2 cup chopped onion	2 packages (9 ounces each)
1 small clove garlic, minced	frozen Italian green beans,
1/2 teaspoon basil leaves,	cooked and drained
crushed	

In skillet, cook bacon until crisp; remove. Brown mushrooms and cook onion with garlic and basil in drippings until tender. Add soup, water, and beans. Heat; stir occasionally. Garnish with bacon. Makes about 4 cups.

CAULIFLOWER AU GRATIN

A creamy white head of cauliflower gets a cheesy coating made from condensed Cheddar cheese soup, sour cream and lemon juice.

1/4 cup sliced green onions	1/4 cup water
1 tablespoon butter or	1/2 cup sour cream
margarine	1 teaspoon lemon juice
1 can (11 ounces) condensed	1 large head cauliflower,
Cheddar cheese soup	cooked and drained

In saucepan, cook onion in butter until tender. Add remaining ingredients except cauliflower. Heat; stir occasionally. Serve over cauliflower. Makes 6 servings.

STUFFED MUSHROOM CAPS

An imaginative vegetable to serve a guest are these cornbread stuffed mushroom "cups."

1 pound large mushrooms	1/4 cup chopped onion
(about 12 to 16)	1/2 teaspoon rosemary leaves,
3 tablespoons butter or	crushed
margarine, melted	1/8 teaspoon poultry seasoning
1/2 cup chopped zucchini	1 can (10 3/4 ounces) condensed
squash	cream of potato soup
1/4 cup shredded carrot	1 cup cornbread stuffing mix

Remove mushroom stems; coarsley chop. Dip caps in melted butter; arrange cap-side down in 2-quart shallow baking dish (12x8x2"). Meanwhile, in saucepan, cook chopped mushrooms, zucchini, carrot, and onion with seasonings in butter until tender. Remove from heat; stir in soup and stuffing mix. Spoon into mushroom caps. Cover; bake at 375°F. for 30 minutes or until done. Makes 3 to 4 servings.

Sumptuous Salads and Salad Dressings

Sumptuous Salads & Salad Dressings

Call them salads, <u>salatts</u> or <u>sallets</u>; they're just plain good eating.

<u>Sallet</u> was the old English word for large numbers of uncooked tender leaves and plants. In Chaucer, there is a reference to a 14th century chap who enjoyed a <u>sallet</u> of "garlic, onions and lettuce." Early American cookbooks included "receipts" for <u>salatts</u> dressed with <u>oyl</u> and vinegar and herbs.

Colonial <u>salatts</u> featured the use of many herbs for flavoring. It was an obvious synergism since most colonial kitchen gardens were planted with a multitude of herbs to be used for home remedies as well as for cooking. The refinement of medical science in the 19th century had an effect on the creativity of salad making, however. As homegrown medicinal herbs were used less and less, fewer herbs were planted and salad flavoring lost out too.

Many people often think primarily of lettuce when they think of salads. Common as it may seem now, lettuce was once the most royal of salad ingredients. A native of the Middle East, lettuce was such a delicacy in that region that its consumption there was reserved solely for Persian kings and noblemen.

The Greeks and Romans were allowed greater accessibility to it. The Greeks enjoyed it at the end of their meals and the Romans used it as a kind of appetizer, perhaps the forerunner of the antipasto. King Henry VIII was so enchanted with lettuce that he awarded a special prize to the gardener who first grew it for him.

Lettuce seeds were among the first seeds sown by colonists in this country, and Thomas Jefferson carried on the practice in his gardens. He grew about 20 varieties in addition to other salad ingredients like tomatoes, parsley, radishes, cucumbers, celery and cabbage.

Today's choice of salad greens is extensive, so take advantage of the greenery available. Iceberg, romaine, Bibb, leaf, Boston. They're only the beginning. Go on to experiment with endive, chickory, watercress, escarole, Chinese cabbage and early spring dandelion greens.

Though green salad may be the oldest kind, the term, salad, is used to cover many other combinations of food, including certain kinds of elegant molds. Fruit, chicken and seafood mixed with appropriate dressings and seasonings have been served as salads since the end of the 18th century.

Salads are adaptable and versatile enough to be used in a variety of ways. In some areas, they are served between the soup course and the entree; or sometimes with the entree. They can be garnished inventively and often are dramatic centerpieces at a buffet dinner. They can be a sophisticated surprise at a tailgate picnic or a refreshing main course for luncheon or a light supper.

For most salads, the dressing is vital. Sometimes, it is a tart contrast to the salad ingredients; other times mellow, or sweet, or highly seasoned depending on the salad itself. There are many kinds of salad molds, two of which are pictured on the preceding page. One is a Ham Hawaiian Ring. This is dramatic in appearance and is an interesting medley of textures and flavors. To make it, ham slices line a mold which is filled with a colorful rice mixture that includes pineapple, celery, pimiento and green onion. Condensed cream of chicken soup is used to bind the rice combination. A piquant sauce is served with it.

The other mold illustrated here uses gelatine and chicken broth to hold the traditional Gazpacho ingredients in solid form. The result is a new variation on the delicious cold and highly seasoned Spanish favorite.

Crab Louis is shown as the filling in the avocado half. It is a good example of a substantial, elegant, but simple-to-assemble salad. The key to this sumptuous dish lies in the tangy dressing for the crab. Its base is tomato soup blended with mayonnaise and spiced with horseradish, lemon juice, onion and Worcestershire sauce.

The Glazed Cold Buffet to the left in the picture offers an interesting way to serve cold meats. Condensed consomme is used in the gelatine glaze for added flavor.

There are as many variations of salad dressings as there are salads. The root of the word salad is sal, the Latin word for salt, probably the first salad dressing. Since then, there have been countless numbers, each with its own charms.

Oil and vinegar still head the list in the classic, basic vinaigrette dressing. The usual proportions of vinegar to oil are one to three, but there are other variations depending on personal taste. Sometimes lemon juice is substituted for vinegar. Salt, pepper, herbs and condiments can be added.

Then, there are the dressings based on that 17th century invention, mayonnaise, which came into being shortly after a French victory over the English at Port Mahon (mahonaise). In the past 300 years, mayonnaise has provided the base for many interesting dressings. One golden garlic version, aioli, is so popular in the French countryside that whole villages celebrate with a day of feasting called "Le Grand Aioli." On that day, mounds of fresh vegetables, fish and eggs are set out to be dipped in this piquant sauce. Russian, Thousand Island, Green Goddess, Lamaze dressings are other kinds of mayonnaise based dressings with distinctive flavor characteristics.

Boiled salad dressing offers another interesting alternative. These have an egg base and are particularly good with vegetable salads.

Whatever your choice in salad dressing, keep in mind that condensed soups can ease your preparation time considerably while adding sparkle to the flavor. Mayonnaise dressings are great made with a base of either cream of celery soup or cream of mushroom soup. Superior vinaigrette dressings can be made with a base of condensed tomato soup as in the Tomato Italian Dressing.

John Evelyn penned a description in the 17th century of an ideal salad and it still holds true today:

"In the composure of a Sallet, every plant should
come in to bear its part without being overpowered
by some herb of a stronger taste but should fall
into its place like notes in music."

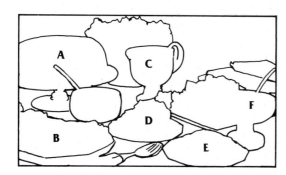

A HAM HAWAIIAN RING
B GLAZED COLD BUFFET
C TOMATO VINAIGRETTE
D CRAB LOUIS
E GAZPACHO MOLD
F PATIO SALAD

CALICO SALAD

An assortment of vegetables and meat strips give this salad its patterned appearance once it is combined with a lightly flavored curry dressing.

1 can (10 3/4 ounces) condensed cream of celery soup
1/2 cup sour cream
1/2 cup water
1 tablespoon chopped chutney
1 teaspoon curry powder

1 teaspoon lime or lemon juice
2 packages (10 ounces each) frozen mixed vegetables, cooked and drained
1 1/2 cups cooked tongue or ham cut in strips

To make dressing, in saucepan, combine soup, sour cream, water, chutney, curry powder, and lime juice. Bring to boil; reduce heat. Simmer a few minutes to blend flavors. Toss with remaining ingredients; chill. Serve on salad greens. Makes about 8 cups.

BEEF BRITTANY

Welcome on a hot summer day — a shimmering salad mold with chunks of meat, cheese and vegetables.

2 envelopes unflavored gelatine
1 1/2 cups cold water
2 cans (10 1/2 ounces each) condensed consomme
5 teaspoons bottled meat sauce
1 cup cooked beef cut in thin strips

1/2 cup crumbled blue cheese
1/2 cup diced green pepper
1/4 cup sliced green onions
2 tablespoons finely chopped pimiento

In saucepan, sprinkle gelatine on cold water to soften. Place over low heat, stirring until gelatine is dissolved. Remove from heat; stir in consomme and meat sauce. Chill until slightly thickened. Fold in remaining ingredients. Pour into 6-cup mold. Chill until firm. Unmold on salad greens. Makes about 5 1/2 cups.

CRAB LOUIS

A west coast favorite that travelled east many years ago. Avocado shells piled high with the crab mixture are tempting at lunchtime.

1 can (10 3/4 ounces) condensed tomato soup
1/4 cup mayonnaise
1/2 cup chopped green pepper
1/4 cup chopped dill pickle
1/4 cup finely chopped onion
3 tablespoons prepared horseradish

2 tablespoons lemon juice
1 tablespoon Worcestershire
1 pound well-drained cooked Alaskan King crab meat (about 2 cups)
3 medium avocados, cut in half

Blend soup and mayonnaise. Add green pepper, pickle, onion, horseradish, lemon juice, Worcestershire, and crab; chill. Spoon into avocado halves. Arrange on salad greens; garnish with lemon wedges. Makes about 4 1/2 cups.

GLAZED COLD BUFFET

The sparkling glaze on this cold buffet platter consists of condensed consomme, gelatine and mild seasonings. When the glaze and foods are eaten together it's paradise.

1 envelope unflavored gelatine
1/2 cup cold water
1 can (10 1/2 ounces)
    condensed consomme
1 teaspoon vinegar
2 teaspoons grated onion
1/4 teaspoon Worcestershire
3 servings sliced cooked ham
    or tongue

3 servings sliced cooked chicken
1 hard-cooked egg, sliced
1 package (10 ounces) frozen
    broccoli flowerets, cooked and
    well-drained
Sliced pimiento-stuffed olives

In saucepan, sprinkle gelatine on cold water to soften. Place over low heat, stirring until gelatine is dissolved. Remove from heat; stir in consomme, vinegar, onion, and Worcestershire. Chill until slightly thickened. Meanwhile, on large serving platter (12 × 9″), arrange remaining ingredients. Spoon a thin layer of gelatine mixture over the entire platter. Chill until set. Makes 6 servings.

PATIO SALAD

A blender-smooth dressing of mushroom soup, cheese, preserves and lime juice binds the fruits and chicken in this chilled salad.

1 can (10 1/2 ounces) condensed
    cream of mushroom soup
1 package (3 ounces) cream
    cheese, softened
1/4 cup milk
3 tablespoons apricot preserves
1 tablespoon lime juice

1 large honeydew melon, cut in
    cubes
2 cups blueberries
2 cups strawberries,
    cut in half
1 1/2 cups cubed cooked chicken

To make salad dressing, in blender, combine soup, cream cheese, milk, preserves, and lime juice. Blend until smooth; chill. Toss remaining ingredients. Serve on salad greens with dressing. Garnish fruit with mint. Makes 4 servings.

CRUNCHY CUCUMBER SALAD

If you purchase cucumbers with a shiny waxed coating be sure to pare them. Otherwise cut them into thin rounds with a green border.

1 can (10 3/4 ounces) condensed
    cream of celery soup
1/2 cup sour cream
2 tablespoons finely chopped
    onion

1/4 cup chopped radishes
Generous dash pepper
4 cups thinly sliced cucumbers
    (about 4 medium)

Combine soup, sour cream, onion, radishes, and pepper. Add cucumbers; chill. Serve on salad greens; garnish with parsley and additional radishes. Makes about 4 cups.

DIAMOND HEAD CHICKEN SALAD

A salad worth the last forkful because the chicken is in chunks. Pineapple, apple and Macadamia nuts are tossed with it in a curry dressing.

1 can (10 3/4 ounces) condensed cream of chicken soup
1/2 cup water
2 tablespoons chopped parsley
1 teaspoon lemon juice
1/2 teaspoon curry powder
1 small head lettuce, torn in bite-size pieces (about 8 cups)

1 small pineapple, cut in chunks (about 3 cups)
1 medium apple, diced (about 1 cup)
2 cans (5 ounces each) chunk white chicken or 2 cups cooked shrimp cut up
2 tablespoons chopped Macadamia nuts

To make dressing, combine soup, water, parsley, lemon juice, and curry; chill. Toss lightly with remaining ingredients. Makes about 9 cups.

MOLDED SHRIMP SALAD

A delicious molded seafood salad for a summer luncheon. Unmold it onto a bed of mixed greens . . . bite-size pieces of romaine, escarole and iceberg lettuce.

2 cans (7 ounces each) shrimp
2 envelopes unflavored gelatine
1 1/2 cups cold water
1 can (10 3/4 ounces) condensed tomato soup

1 package (8 ounces) cream cheese
1/2 cup sour cream
1 1/2 cups chopped celery
1/3 cup sliced green onions

Drain shrimp, reserving 1/3 cup liquid. In saucepan, sprinkle gelatine on water to soften; add soup, cream cheese, and reserved shrimp liquid. Place over low heat, stirring until gelatine is dissolved and cream cheese is melted. Gradually stir into sour cream. Chill until slightly thickened. Fold in remaining ingredients. Pour into 6-cup mold. Chill until firm. Unmold on salad greens. Makes about 5 cups.

BLUE RIBBON CARROT SALAD

A layered salad of onion, green pepper and cooked carrot slices marinates in a sweet and sour tomato soup dressing. Serve it well chilled with roast beef.

2 pounds medium carrots, sliced (about 6 cups)
1 can (10 3/4 ounces) condensed tomato soup
1 cup sugar
3/4 cup vinegar

1/2 cup salad oil
1 teaspoon dry mustard
1 teaspoon Worcestershire
1 medium onion, sliced
1 medium green pepper, cut in strips

In saucepan, cook carrots in salted water until tender; drain. Meanwhile, to make marinade, combine soup, sugar, vinegar, salad oil, mustard, and Worcestershire. In shallow dish, arrange alternate layers of onion, pepper, and carrots. Pour marinade over all; refrigerate 6 hours or more. Makes about 6 cups.

CALIFORNIA SALAD

The blandness of avocado requires a zippy dressing. Add orange juice to tomato soup, plus the usual oil and vinegar, for a California-style dressing.

1 can (10 3/4 ounces) condensed tomato soup
3/4 cup orange juice
1/2 cup salad oil
1/4 cup vinegar
2 tablespoons finely chopped onion
6 cups lettuce torn into bite-size pieces

4 slices bacon, cooked and crumbled
1 medium avocado, sliced
1 cup sliced onion
1 cup green pepper squares
1/4 cup sliced ripe olives

To make dressing, in jar or shaker, combine soup, orange juice, oil, vinegar, and chopped onion; chill. Shake well before using. In large bowl, toss remaining ingredients. Serve with dressing. Makes about 8 cups.

CREAMY COLE SLAW

Such a cinch to make this smoothest of dressings with cream of celery soup. If you own a food processor use it for the vegetables.

1 can (10 3/4 ounces) condensed cream of celery soup
1/4 cup mayonnaise
1/2 teaspoon caraway seed

6 cups cabbage cut in long thin shreds
1/2 cup chopped green pepper
1/4 cup chopped green onions

In bowl, blend soup, mayonnaise, and caraway. Toss with remaining ingredients; chill. Serve on salad greens; garnish with green pepper rings. Makes about 5 cups.

DILLED POTATO SALAD

Fresh dill has a lovely aroma and distinctive taste. Chop some into your soup-based dressing for potato salad.

1 can (10 3/4 ounces) condensed cream of celery soup
1/2 cup sour cream
1 tablespoon vinegar
1/4 cup chopped onion
2 tablespoons chopped fresh dill or 2 teaspoons dried dill weed, crushed

1/4 teaspoon salt
Dash pepper
4 cups cubed cooked potatoes
1 cup shredded carrot

Combine soup, sour cream, vinegar, onion, and seasonings. Add potatoes and carrot; chill. Serve on salad greens. Makes about 5 cups.

EMERALD VEGETABLE RING

In place of the usual greens in a salad, choose bright green, well formed romaine leaves, cook them and line your ring mold. Then fill with salad; cover and chill.

8 large romaine lettuce leaves	1/4 cup chopped green onions
1 can (10 3/4 ounces) condensed cream of celery soup	1/4 cup chopped pimiento
3 packages (10 ounces each) frozen peas and carrots, cooked and drained	2 tablespoons prepared horseradish
	2 tablespoons vinegar
2 cups cooked rice	1 tablespoon Dijon mustard
1/3 cup chopped water chestnuts	1/2 teaspoon salt
	Generous dash pepper

Cook romaine in water a few minutes to soften; drain. Line a 6 1/2-cup ring mold with romaine leaves, overlapping leaves to completely cover mold. Combine remaining ingredients. Pack mixture into romaine-lined mold. Cover with waxed paper; chill. To serve, invert on serving platter. Makes 8 to 10 servings.

GAZPACHO MOLD

Fresh vegetables make this a colorful, crunchy salad even though it's molded in a gelatine-chicken broth base.

2 envelopes unflavored gelatine	Dash cayenne pepper
1/2 cup cold water	2 cups chopped fresh tomatoes
2 cans (10 3/4 ounces each) condensed chicken broth	1 cup chopped cucumber
	1/2 cup chopped green pepper
1/8 teaspoon garlic powder	1/4 cup finely chopped onion

In saucepan, sprinkle gelatine on cold water to soften. Place over low heat, stirring until gelatine is dissolved. Remove from heat; add broth and seasonings. Chill until slightly thickened. Fold in remaining ingredients. Pour into 8-cup mold or 8 individual molds. Chill until firm. Unmold on salad greens. Makes about 6 1/2 cups.

SPINACH SALAD A LA RUSSE

Colorful additions to the ever-popular spinach salad make this a meal-in-one bowl. It's excellent with the creamy tomato-horseradish dressing.

1 can (10 3/4 ounces) condensed tomato soup	4 hard-cooked eggs, sliced
1/2 cup sour cream	2 cans (3 3/4 ounces each) sardines, drained
1/4 cup milk	1 cup sliced cucumber
2 teaspoons prepared horseradish	1/2 cup sliced red onion
8 cups spinach torn in bite-size pieces	1/2 cup sweet gherkin pickles cut in strips

To make dressing, blend soup, sour cream, milk, and horseradish; chill. In large bowl, layer remaining ingredients. Serve with dressing. Makes 4 servings.

TOMATO SHRIMP BASKETS

Leftover chicken or shrimp? Make it special with tarragon, mayonnaise, eggs and vegetables combined to fill tomato cups.

1 can (10 3/4 ounces) condensed
  cream of chicken soup
1/4 cup mayonnaise
1/2 teaspoon salt
1/8 teaspoon tarragon leaves,
  crushed
2 cups cut up cooked shrimp
  or cubed cooked chicken

2 hard-cooked eggs, chopped
1/2 cup chopped celery
1/2 cup chopped green pepper
2 tablespoons thinly sliced green
  onions
6 medium tomatoes
Salt
Pepper

In bowl, blend soup, mayonnaise, 1/2 teaspoon salt, and tarragon. Stir in shrimp, eggs, celery, green pepper, and onions; chill. Place tomatoes stem end down. With knife, cut each tomato almost to stem end, making 5 or 6 sections; spread apart slightly. Season with salt and pepper; fill with shrimp mixture. Arrange on salad greens. Makes 6 servings.

HAM HAWAIIAN RING

A delightful combination of ham, pineapple and rice molded into a ring. Gingered sour cream sauce tops it off in Hawaiian-style.

1 pound thinly sliced boiled ham
  (about 16 slices)
1 can (10 3/4 ounces) condensed
  cream of chicken soup
1/3 cup mayonnaise
4 cups unsalted cooked rice
1 cup drained crushed pineapple
  in pure pineapple juice

1/2 cup chopped celery
1/4 cup drained chopped pimiento
3 tablespoons chopped green
  onions
1/4 teaspoon ground ginger

Line a 6 1/2-cup ring mold with half the ham, overlapping slices to completely cover mold. Finely chop remaining ham; set aside.

To make filling: In bowl, blend soup and mayonnaise; stir in chopped ham and remaining ingredients. Pack mixture into ham-lined mold. Cover with waxed paper; chill overnight.

To make sauce: In small bowl, combine the following ingredients; chill:

1/2 cup mayonnaise
1/2 cup sour cream
1/2 cup drained crushed pineapple
  in pure pineapple juice

1/4 teaspoon ground ginger

To unmold: Carefully run spatula around insides of mold; invert on serving platter. Serve with sauce. Makes 4 to 6 servings.

LIGHT AND COOL CUCUMBER SALAD

The flavors of lemon and dill highlight this molded salad which is marvelous to serve at a noon luncheon.

1/2 cup boiling water
1 package (3 ounces)
    lemon-flavored gelatin
1 can (10 3/4 ounces) condensed
    cream of celery soup
1 package (8 ounces) cream
    cheese, softened

1/2 teaspoon dried dill weed
1 cup chopped cucumber
1 cup chopped radishes
1/4 cup sliced green onions
1/4 cup chopped green pepper

In bowl, pour water over gelatin; stir until dissolved. Chill until slightly thickened. Beat with rotary beater or electric mixer until fluffy and about double in volume. Meanwhile, gradually blend soup into cheese and dill weed until smooth. Gradually fold soup mixture and remaining ingredients into gelatin. Chill until firm. Serve on slices of cucumber. Makes about 4 cups.

CHICKEN SALAD A LA ORANGE

Family and friends alike will love this new taste sensation. Chicken and grapes abound in the salad. Sprinkle with almonds. Serve with orange dressing.

1 can (10 3/4 ounces) condensed
    cream of chicken soup
1/2 cup orange juice
    concentrate
1 tablespoon honey
1/4 teaspoon grated orange rind
1 medium head romaine lettuce,
    torn in bite-size pieces
    (about 8 cups)

2 cups cooked chicken cut in
    strips
1 cup seedless white grapes cut
    in half
1/2 cup toasted slivered almonds

To make dressing, combine soup, orange juice concentrate, honey, and orange rind; chill. Toss lightly with remaining ingredients. Garnish with additional almonds. Makes about 8 cups.

PIQUANT SALAD DRESSINGS

A versatile dressing for many types of salads ... from hot potato to tossed vegetable salads.

1 can (10 3/4 ounces) condensed cream of celery soup	1 teaspoon sugar
	1/4 teaspoon salt
3 eggs	Dash cayenne pepper
1/4 cup vinegar	1 1/2 cups salad oil
1 teaspoon dry mustard	

In blender, combine all ingredients except oil. Cover; blend on high speed a few seconds. With blender <u>still</u> on high speed, remove cover. <u>Very slowly</u> pour oil in a steady stream into soup mixture. Chill. Makes about 4 cups basic salad dressing.

<u>Blue Cheese Sour Cream Dressing</u>: Gradually stir 1 cup basic salad dressing into 2 tablespoons sour cream. Add 1/4 cup crumbled blue cheese; chill. Serve on salad greens, baked potatoes, hamburgers, or vegetable salads. Makes about 1 cup.

<u>Green Goddess Dressing</u>: Combine 1 cup basic salad dressing, 1 tablespoon chopped anchovy fillets, 1 tablespoon finely chopped parsley, and 1/4 teaspoon tarragon leaves, crushed. Chill. Serve on salad greens. Makes about 1 cup.

EAST INDIA DRESSING

A zesty sauce for seafood ... shrimp, crab or lobster. Or, serve it in a sauce boat as an accompaniment to broiled white fish fillets.

1 can (10 3/4 ounces) condensed tomato soup	2 tablespoons chopped green pepper
1/2 cup chopped chutney	1/8 teaspoon hot pepper sauce
1/2 cup mayonnaise	

In bowl, combine ingredients. Chill. Serve with cooked seafood. Makes about 2 cups.

YOGURT BLUE CHEESE DRESSING

Attention blue cheese lovers! A creamy dressing mingled with crumbled blue cheese and crunchy onions and cucumber is a must for you to try.

1 can (10 3/4 ounces) condensed cream of celery soup	1/4 cup crumbled blue cheese
	1 tablespoon finely chopped onion
1 cup chopped cucumber	1/2 teaspoon vinegar
1 cup plain yogurt	

In bowl, combine ingredients. Chill. Serve on salad greens. Makes about 3 cups.

TOMATO ITALIAN DRESSING

Herbs in leaf form should be crushed for maximum flavor when used in dressings. Note how well they permeate this tomato soup dressing.

1 can (10 3/4 ounces) condensed tomato soup
1/2 cup salad or olive oil
1/4 cup vinegar
1/4 cup grated Parmesan cheese

1 teaspoon basil leaves, crushed
1 teaspoon oregano leaves, crushed
1/8 teaspoon garlic salt

In covered jar or shaker, combine ingredients; chill. Shake well before using. Makes about 2 cups.

LEMON CHIFFON DRESSING

A fresh fruit bowl, consisting of sliced peaches, hulled strawberries, orange sections and banana chunks, takes kindly to a light lemon dressing.

1 can (10 3/4 ounces) condensed tomato soup

1/3 cup lemonade concentrate
1/2 cup heavy cream, whipped

Combine soup and lemonade. Gradually fold into whipped cream; chill. Serve with assorted fresh fruit. Makes about 2 cups.

TOMATO VINAIGRETTE

There are many variations of the basic vinaigrette dressing but this recipe is unique with its tomato soup and spicy seasonings. Pour it onto a bowl of mixed greens.

1 can (10 3/4 ounces) condensed tomato soup
1/2 cup salad oil
1/4 cup vinegar

2 teaspoons grated onion
1/2 teaspoon chili powder
1/8 teaspoon hot sauce

In covered jar or shaker, combine ingredients; chill. Shake well before using. Makes about 1 1/2 cups.

CAESAR SALAD DRESSING

Obviously the dressing for salad of the same name, but try it on spinach salad, too.

1 can (10 3/4 ounces) condensed cream of mushroom soup
1/2 cup salad oil

1/4 cup lemon juice
1 teaspoon anchovy paste
Generous dash garlic powder

In covered jar or shaker, combine soup, oil, lemon juice, anchovy paste, and garlic powder; chill. Shake well before using. Makes about 1 1/2 cups.

Noble Sauces

Noble Sauces

For centuries, saucemaking has been a pinnacle of a chef's culinary achievement. Starting as apprentice sauciers, chefs learn practical basics, progress to the fine points, then create new flavors and perfect their art. Having reached that goal, they enjoy considerable esteem.

The evolution of saucemaking can be traced back through many centuries. Greco-Roman culinary techniques recommended preserving natural food flavors by cooking food in its own juices, then enriching its flavors with a sauce made from stock seasoned with spices, wine and garnishes. Garum was the basic Roman sauce made from fermented fish and seasoned with wine or vinegar and spices such as cumin, cardamom and coriander.

New spices brought back to Europe by returning Crusaders contributed a whole new dimension to early sauces. Cinnamon, mustard, ginger and saffron became popular as flavorings in the 14th century. Tallievent, author of the oldest French cookbook on record, Le Viandier, published around 1375, used them extensively in his recipes. Moreover, he was quite preoccupied with the art of fine saucemaking and included recipes for 17 different sauces in his book.

The dawn of classic French cuisine and thus the classic sauces are recognized as occurring in 1553 with the arrival of Catherine de Medici at the French court of Francis I. Catherine had come to marry Francis' son, the future Henry II, and her entourage included Italian chefs, then considered to be the finest in Europe. She also brought with her the enlightened culinary refinements that Italy had enjoyed for a few hundred years. From the throne, through the court and down into the aristocracy, these new ideas revolutionized French kitchens.

Over the next 500 years, a superior cuisine was developed and refined. Names like La Varenne, De Lunne, Massaliot, La Chapelle, Mirepoix read like a litany for classic sauce devotees. But it was Marie-Antoine Careme who gave purity and order to the art. He proposed the "mother sauce" concept. Simply, the concept suggested that with the addition of an infinite variety of seasonings, almost all other sauces could be made from a basic three. Not at all modest in his achievements, he wrote in his book, Le Cuisinier Parisien in 1828, "Be aware that no foreign sauce is comparable to those of our great modern cuisine."

Classic sauces have stood the test of time and Careme's approach to learning the basics still holds true. Mastery of the fundamental white, brown and emulsified sauces is the place to start.

The first important step in making white and brown sauces is in understanding the <u>roux</u>, a careful blending and cooking of flour and fat. Then liquid is added. Patience with this process is a necessity in order to avoid a floury taste in the finished product. Proper timing and exact proportions are also essential.

The white sauces, or bechamels and veloutes, have as their foundations the blonde roux and are basically the same. However, bechamel uses milk as the hot liquid, while veloute uses a meat stock. Various flavor enrichments to either of these basic sauces can include herbs, spices, cheese or wine for completely new variations.

Classic espagnole or brown sauces are based on a demi-glace, or reduced stock. This stock is the product of long term simmering of veal, beef, vegetables, condiments and wine. A true demi-glace requires many steps and often two days of simmering of the ingredients, but the results are superb. Other brown sauces are prepared from a roux made from browned flours and are usually seasoned heartily. A less complicated brown sauce is produced by deglazing a roasting pan or skillet in which the food has been cooked.

The emulsified sauces are a suspension of oil or butter and flavoring in an egg base. These require very little or no cooking and include mayonnaise, Hollandaise and its more piquant sister, Bearnaise.

Various other sauces fall into no particular category. They include marinades, tomato, butter, barbecue and dessert sauces.

The purpose of a sauce is not only to impart new taste but to enhance and enrich flavors characteristic of the food with which it will be used. Sensitivity to this fine balance and blending is a prerequisite for a saucier, as well as knowledge of seasonings and the willingness to experiment.

You don't have to be a master saucier to recreate the recipes in this chapter. Traditionals like Perigourdine, Toulonnaise and Mornay get a head start using condensed soups as the base. To produce the stock for the Perigourdine, shown in the photograph, use condensed golden mushroom soup as the starting point for it is a ready-to-use, blended mixture of beef stock, mushrooms and seasonings. Shallots, truffles, Madeira wine, tomato paste and seasonings complete this distinctive sauce.

In the center of the same photograph, elegant Mornay sauce adds the crowning touch to the asparagus. All you need to produce this excellent touch is a can of condensed cream of chicken soup, cheeses, white wine and an egg. The Tartar sauce shown with fish fillets is great with other seafood too. You will use it often after you taste the excellent results produced from combining cream of celery soup and mayonnaise laced with India relish, grated onion and lemon juice.

For serious pasta fanciers, the Spaghetti Sauce Abruzzi is a rare phenomenon, a richly spiced but mellow spaghetti sauce that simmers for just 30 minutes. The rich English Mustard Sauce so proper with baked ham evokes memories of lavish banquets in Edwardian England.

Mastering the art of fine saucemaking is made considerably easier by using condensed soups. One need not spend a lifetime perfecting the technique. Soups reduce the preparation time and can be relied upon for a consistent base. Seasonings, then in Careme's infinite wisdom, make the difference. The recipes here are an introduction to fine sauces, which once tried, can greatly expand the pleasures of cooking and enjoying good food.

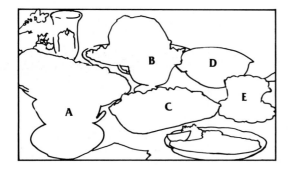

A PERIGOURDINE SAUCE
B ENGLISH MUSTARD SAUCE
C MORNAY SAUCE
D SPAGHETTI SAUCE ABRUZZI
E MOCK TARTAR SAUCE

BARBECUE SAUCE AU VIN

Male cooks take pride in a good barbecue sauce for chicken or beef. Order these ingredients, then offer them with the recipe to the presiding chef.

2 tablespoons chopped onion
1 medium clove garlic, minced
2 tablespoons salad oil
1 can (10 3/4 ounces) condensed
   tomato soup
1/3 cup chablis or other dry
   white wine

2 teaspoons brown sugar
2 teaspoons lemon juice
1 teaspoon Worcestershire
1/4 teaspoon hot pepper sauce

In saucepan, cook onion with garlic in oil until tender. Add remaining ingredients. Bring to boil; reduce heat. Simmer 10 minutes; stir occasionally. Use as a barbecue sauce for chicken or beef. Makes about 1 1/2 cups.

TOULONNAISE SAUCE

An easy-to-prepare sauce with capers and ripe olives. Serve hot in a sauce boat to spoon over cooked salmon or halibut.

2 tablespoons sliced green
   onions
1 tablespoon butter or
   margarine
1 can (10 3/4 ounces) condensed
   cream of celery soup

1/3 cup milk
2 tablespoons chablis or other
   dry white wine
1 tablespoon chopped capers
1 tablespoon chopped ripe olives

In saucepan, cook onions in butter until tender; add remaining ingredients. Heat; stir occasionally. Serve over cooked fish. Makes about 2 cups.

ORANGE MUSTARD SAUCE

Orange juice and Dijon (French) mustard heighten the flavor of cream of chicken soup in a sauce for roast leg of lamb or ham.

1/4 cup chopped green pepper
1 tablespoon butter or
   margarine
1 can (10 3/4 ounces) condensed
   cream of chicken soup

1/4 cup orange juice
2 tablespoons Dijon mustard

In saucepan, cook green pepper in butter until tender. Add remaining ingredients. Heat; stir occasionally. Serve over cooked ham or lamb. Makes about 1 1/2 cups.

MORNAY SAUCE

Two cheeses ... Gruyere and Parmesan ... help make Mornay Sauce authentic. A perfect for asparagus.

1 can (10 3/4 ounces) condensed cream of chicken soup
1/2 cup milk
1/3 cup sauterne or other dry white wine

1/2 cup shredded process Gruyere cheese
1 tablespoon grated Parmesan cheese
1 egg, slightly beaten

In saucepan, combine ingredients. Cook, stirring until thickened. Serve over cooked vegetables. Makes about 2 1/2 cups.

SPAGHETTI SAUCE ABRUZZI

Italians from the southern towns of Italy, such as Abruzzi, make excellent meatless spaghetti sauces. See for yourself when you try this recipe.

1/3 cup very finely chopped onion
1/4 teaspoon basil leaves, crushed
1/8 teaspoon thyme leaves, crushed
1 small clove garlic, minced
1 tablespoon butter or margarine

1 tablespoon olive oil
1 can (10 3/4 ounces) condensed tomato soup
1 can (about 6 ounces) tomato paste
1 soup can water
2 tablespoons grated Parmesan cheese
1/2 teaspoon salt
1/2 small bay leaf
Cooked spaghetti

In saucepan, cook onion with basil, thyme, and garlic in butter and oil until tender. Blend in remaining ingredients except spaghetti. Bring to boil; reduce heat. Simmer 30 minutes; stir occasionally. Serve with spaghetti. Makes about 2 1/2 cups.

NEWBURG SAUCE

Cream and sherry blend well with cream of shrimp soup. With buttery mushrooms in the sauce it's a pleasure to serve it with cooked shellfish.

1 cup sliced fresh mushrooms (about 1/4 pound)
2 tablespoons butter or margarine

1 can (10 3/4 ounces) condensed cream of shrimp soup
1/4 cup light cream
1/4 cup sherry

In saucepan, brown mushrooms in butter. Add remaining ingredients. Heat; stir occasionally. Serve over cooked shrimp or lobster. Makes about 1 1/2 cups.

SAUCE SOUBISE

A very old recipe for Sauce Soubise reveals a complicated method for preparing the onions. No problems exist in this recipe. Serve it over cooked string beans.

1 cup finely chopped onion
1/4 cup butter or margarine
1 can (11 ounces) condensed
   Cheddar cheese soup

1/2 cup milk

In saucepan, cook onion in butter until tender. Stir in soup and milk. Heat; stir occasionally. Serve over cooked vegetables. Makes about 2 cups.

PERIGOURDINE SAUCE

Without truffles and Madeira wine this sauce would not be classic. Since they are included in this recipe, we suggest you splurge and serve it over filet of beef.

1 can (1/2 ounce) truffles
1 tablespoon finely chopped
   shallots
Generous dash crushed thyme
   leaves
1 tablespoon butter or
   margarine

1 can (10 3/4 ounces) condensed
   golden mushroom soup
1 tablespoon dry Madeira wine
   (golden)
1 tablespoon tomato paste
1 small bay leaf

Drain truffles, reserving liquid; dice. In saucepan, cook shallots with thyme in butter until tender. Add truffles, reserved liquid, and remaining ingredients. Heat; stir occasionally. Remove bay leaf. Serve over filet of beef. Makes about 1 cup.

EASY BEARNAISE SAUCE

Shallots, tarragon and dry white wine incorporated into cream of celery soup will result in an easy variation of the classic Bearnaise.

2 tablespoons finely chopped
   onion or shallots
2 tablespoons chopped parsley
Generous dash crushed
   tarragon leaves
2 tablespoons butter or
   margarine

2 tablespoons sauterne or other
   dry white wine
1 can (10 3/4 ounces) condensed
   cream of celery soup
1/3 cup milk

In saucepan, cook onion with parsley and tarragon in butter until tender. Add wine; simmer a few minutes. Stir in soup and milk. Heat; stir occasionally. Serve over cooked beef or ham. Makes about 1 1/2 cups.

MOCK TARTAR SAUCE

Whip up a mock tartar sauce in minutes with just five ingredients. Two of them, cream of celery soup and mayonnaise blend the sauce together.

1 can (10 3/4 ounces) condensed
    cream of celery soup
1/4 cup mayonnaise

1/4 cup India relish
2 teaspoons grated onion
1 teaspoon lemon juice

In bowl, combine ingredients. Chill. Serve over cooked fish. Makes about 1 1/2 cups.

VENETO BEEF SAUCE

An Italian-inspired sauce for cooked beef. Chianti, a red wine, mellows with the beefy mushroom soup for new flavor.

3 tablespoons Chianti or
    other dry red wine
1 can (10 3/4 ounces) condensed
    beefy mushroom soup

1 tablespoon chopped parsley
1 tablespoon tomato paste

In saucepan, simmer wine a few minutes. Add remaining ingredients. Heat; stir occasionally. Serve over cooked beef. Makes about 1 cup.

CUMBERLAND SAUCE

Sauce your baked ham with this blend of sweet and spicy ingredients — currant jelly, orange juice, wine, mustard and ginger — all heated in condensed chicken broth.

1 can (10 3/4 ounces) condensed
    chicken broth
1/3 cup red currant jelly
1/4 cup orange juice
1/4 cup Port or other sweet
    red wine

2 tablespoons cornstarch
2 tablespoons lemon juice
2 teaspoons dry mustard
1 teaspoon paprika
1/2 teaspoon ground ginger

In saucepan, combine ingredients. Cook, stirring until thickened. Serve over cooked ham or poultry. Makes about 2 cups.

SAVORY BEEF SAUCE

Those friends who like beef rare, medium or well done will welcome a beefy-herb sauce to top each portion.

1 can (10 3/4 ounces) condensed
    beefy mushroom soup
1/4 cup water
1 tablespoon ketchup
1 tablespoon chopped parsley

2 teaspoons Dijon mustard
1/2 teaspoon chervil leaves,
    crushed
1/8 teaspoon tarragon leaves,
    crushed

In saucepan, combine ingredients. Heat; stir occasionally. Serve over cooked beef. Makes about 1 1/2 cups.

ENGLISH MUSTARD SAUCE

A distinctive mustard sauce with generous dashes of cayenne and curry powder. Chopped eggs add a yellow tone.

1 can (10 3/4 ounces) condensed
   cream of celery soup
2 egg yolks
3 tablespoons Dijon mustard
2 tablespoons salad oil
2 tablespoons vinegar
1 tablespoon sugar

2 teaspoons dry mustard
Generous dash cayenne pepper
Dash curry powder
Dash white pepper
2 hard-cooked eggs, chopped
1/2 cup sour cream

In small bowl of electric mixer, combine all ingredients except hard-cooked eggs and sour cream. Beat on high speed until thick (about 3 minutes). Fold in eggs and sour cream. Serve over cooked ham. Makes about 2 1/2 cups.

VIKING CUCUMBER SAUCE

Cucumbers in sauces add a mild flavor. In this creamy herb sauce to serve over fish, you'll find cucumbers add crunch.

1 can (10 3/4 ounces) condensed
   creamy chicken mushroom soup
1/2 cup sour cream
1 tablespoon milk
1 tablespoon lemon juice
1/2 teaspoon celery seed

1/4 teaspoon dried dill weed,
   crushed
1/8 teaspoon savory leaves, crushed
1/2 cup finely chopped cucumber
2 tablespoons finely chopped onion

In bowl, combine soup, sour cream, milk, and seasonings. Add cucumber and onion. Chill 4 hours or more. Serve over cooked fish. Makes about 2 cups.

BLENDER HOLLANDAISE SAUCE

Young cooks, even those with years of experience, often lack confidence in making Hollandaise. With asparagus soup as a stabilizer, make it in a blender.

1 can (10 3/4 ounces) condensed
   cream of asparagus soup
3 egg yolks

2 tablespoons lemon juice
Generous dash hot pepper sauce
1/2 cup butter or margarine, melted

In blender, combine all ingredients except butter. Cover; blend on high speed a few seconds. With blender <u>still</u> on high speed, remove cover. <u>Very slowly</u> pour butter in a steady stream into soup mixture. Blend 3 minutes more or until thick. Serve over cooked fish or vegetables. Makes about 2 cups.

<u>Mousseline Sauce:</u> Prepare as above. Fold in 1/2 cup heavy cream, whipped. Serve over cooked fillet of white fish.

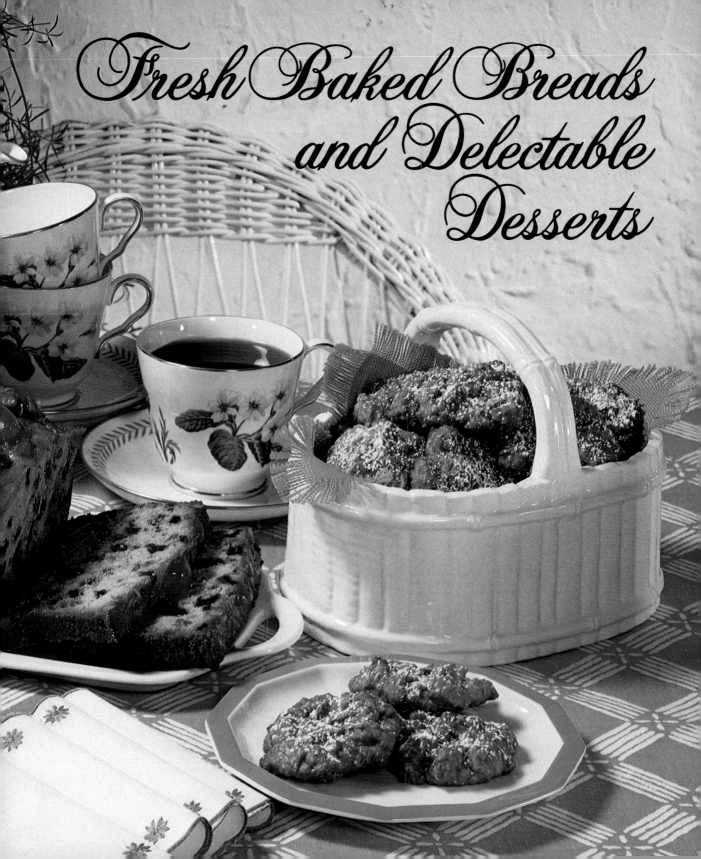

Fresh Baked Breads and Delectable Desserts

Fresh Baked Breads and Delectable Desserts

A romantic mystique permeates the topic of bread-baking. Perhaps it is because bread, the staff of life, has been praised by generations of poets or perhaps it is simply because compelling aromas are associated with golden fresh baked loaves.

Whatever the reasons for the fascination of bread, it has been a major source of food through the great civilizations of the world for almost 9,000 years.

The earliest archeological evidence of bread baking was uncovered in the Middle East at Jericho in the Jordan Valley. There, ovens have been found dating from about 7000 B.C. The primitive bread made in these ovens was not bread as we know it today, however; it was flat, heavy and unleavened.

The Egyptians are credited with having the first yeast-raised bread around 2600 B.C., but there is speculation as to just how they discovered the fermentation process. Some historians believe that wine in which yeast spores were growing was mixed with dough, producing a leavening effect. Others propose that air-born spores of wild yeast, usually present in dusty air, settled on a neglected batch of dough, producing the same results. They also realized that it was possible to perpetuate this magical aeration of dough by merely saving part of each day's dough to impregnate the next batch.

Creativity was the mark of the Egyptian baker. He baked breads in every conceivable shape — round, triangular, conical, spiral, in addition to animal, fish and human forms. Some were even colored with earth pigments while others were flavored with honey, almonds, sweet herbs, fruits and spices. A papyrus dating from about 1200 B.C. lists 30 different kinds of bread being baked in Egypt then.

The Greek civilization was eating leavened bread by about 600 B.C. and even had public bakeries a hundred years later.

The first leavened loaves in the Roman Empire are traced to about 300 B.C. As Rome prospered, the demand for bread increased. Public bakeries flourished from 170 B.C., as women sought ways to avoid the tedious chore of bread baking. Much of the grain was imported from Sicily, Sardinia and Egypt.

While the Egyptians pioneered creativity in bread baking, the Romans specialized in improving the technical aspects of the process. They invented the first mechanical dough mixer, a device that used horses and donkeys walking in a circle to knead the dough. Water-driven mills were also utilized. Such techniques were a necessity, since the Romans were faced with the problem of feeding large numbers of people in the rapidly growing cities. The record of a one mill-bakery in Pompeii dated 79 A.D. shows that 1000 bushels of flour were processed daily to bake between 100,000 and 150,000 loaves of bread.

The first guilds and schools for bakers were formed in the Roman Empire but the concept flourished during the Middle Ages. One such guild, established in London in 1155, The Worshipful Company of Bakers, still exists today.

The legendary term "baker's dozen" dates back to the days of medieval guilds. According to law, German bakers risked punishment in the stocks if they cheated their customers. Rather than be accused of even inadvertently cheating, wise bakers included an extra bun or cake with a purchase, giving birth to the term.

Bread baking in the early American colonies assumed a totally native flavor. Maize was plentiful and easily cultivated and it became the staple grain. Later, Dutch settlers in New York were successful in growing wheat, barley and rye but these finer grains were in relatively short supply and therefore, expensive. It was not until the push to the grain growing prairies of the West that fine milled American flours came into their own.

One indispensible item on the chuck wagon on cattle drives was a crock of sour dough "starter." Trail cooks perpetuated the fermentation of the "starter" in the same manner as the ancient Egyptians, by setting aside a small portion of the raised dough for use in the next batch.

Two factors occuring in the mid-19th century advanced American bread baking to a level never known before. One was the commercial production of baking powder, the other was the progress made in the Midwest milling industry.

Man's quest for sweets somewhat parallels that of bread. Sweets have been sold on the streets by vendors for centuries. The early Egyptians had their favorites which included a kind of marzipan made from crushed almonds and jam. The Greeks feasted on cheese cakes and honey biscuits.

The practice of offering sweets or dessert only at the end of the meal is a fairly recent development. At banquets during the Middle Ages, pastries, blancmanges and custards were served after each course. This sequence was repeated several times during a meal, eventually ending with a sweet.

The use of condensed soup adds a new dimension to the preparation of breads and desserts. This may seem surprising at first, but the results are absolutely delicious. On the preceding page the photograph illustrates several examples.

The Wheat Germ Bread is an old-fashioned loaf with a new-fashioned twist, condensed onion soup. The Pumpkin Oatmeal Cookies heaped in the basket will please even the most discriminating cookie nibbler. They are spicy, full of pumpkin flavor and the subtle richness that condensed potato soup can give.

Among the desserts, the Raspberry Cheese Pie in the foreground made with a base of condensed Cheddar cheese soup, will satisfy the most finicky connoisseur.

The Holiday Fruit Cake with condensed chicken broth as a major liquid ingredient is notably flavorful with fragrant seasonings, crunchy nuts and succulent fruits. The broth helps to enhance the true flavors of all the other ingredients.

For a cold blustery day, a Quick Cheddar Bread, made with biscuit mix, eggs, condensed cream of mushroom soup and, of course, Cheddar cheese, lends an agreeable ambiance to the kitchen and can be the perfect complement to a hot soup and salad.

Home-baking can be one of the real joys in cooking. By all means, bask in the mystique and pleasant aromas knowing that the technique is not so difficult as many assume.

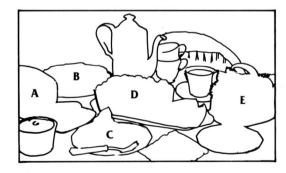

A WHEAT GERM BREAD
B QUICK CHEDDAR BREAD
C RASPBERRY CHEESE PIE
D HOLIDAY FRUITCAKE
E PUMPKIN OATMEAL COOKIES

KUGELHOPF

A German favorite that could easily become one of your most prized recipes. Ground almonds provide the outside coating for this bread.

1 can (10 3/4 ounces) condensed chicken broth	4 eggs
1 package active dry yeast	4 cups all-purpose flour
3/4 cup butter or margarine, softened	1/2 teaspoon salt
3/4 cup sugar	1 1/4 cups golden raisins
	3/4 cup chopped almonds
	1/4 cup ground almonds

Heat chicken broth to lukewarm (110°F.). Sprinkle yeast over broth; stir until dissolved. In large bowl of electric mixer, beat butter and sugar until light and fluffy. Add eggs, one at a time, beating after each addition; scraping sides and bottom of bowl constantly. Add yeast mixture; blend. Add flour and salt; beat on low speed until smooth. Stir in raisins and chopped almonds. Butter large Kugelhopf mold (or 10-cup Turk's Head mold); sprinkle with ground almonds, tilting pan to coat bottom and sides. Pour batter into pan. Cover; let rise in warm place until 1/4-inch from top of pan (about 2 hours). Bake at 375°F. for 1 hour 15 minutes or until done. Remove from pan; cool.

ORANGE BREAD

The aroma of freshly baked orange bread brings everyone to the kitchen. Keep an eye on the loaves as they cool. They might disappear with the bread knife and butter.

6 1/2 to 7 cups sifted all-purpose flour	1 cup water
2 packages active dry yeast	1/2 cup orange juice
3 tablespoons sugar	3 tablespoons butter or margarine
1 tablespoon salt	1 tablespoon grated orange rind
1 can (10 3/4 ounces) condensed cream of mushroom soup	2 teaspoons grated lemon rind
	1 egg, slightly beaten

In large bowl, combine 3 cups flour, yeast, sugar, and salt. In saucepan, combine soup, water, orange juice, butter, and rind. Heat to lukewarm (110°F.); add to dry ingredients. Beat at low speed of electric mixer 30 seconds, scraping bottom and sides of bowl often. Beat at high speed 3 minutes. Stir in remaining flour to make a stiff dough. On lightly floured board, knead dough until smooth (about 10 minutes). Place in greased bowl, turning once. Cover; let rise in warm place until doubled (about 1 hour). Punch down. Cover; let rest 10 minutes. Divide dough in half. Shape each half into a loaf. Place each in a greased loaf pan (9×5×3″). Cover; let rise until doubled (about 1 hour). Brush tops of loaves with egg. Bake at 400°F. for 30 minutes or until done. Remove from pans; cool.

VIENNESE SWEET BREAD

A spiced, fruity bread you'll be proud to serve during the holidays. Lemon glaze has a lovely sheen.

Dough:
5 1/4 cups all-purpose flour

2 packages active dry yeast

1/2 cup sugar

1 can (10 1/2 ounces) condensed consomme

1 teaspoon butter or margarine

2 eggs, slightly beaten

Filling:
2 cups finely chopped almonds (1/2 pound)

2 cups finely chopped walnuts (1/2 pound)

1 cup finely chopped raisins

1 cup packed light brown sugar

3 eggs, slightly beaten

1/3 cup butter or margarine, melted

1 tablespoon grated lemon rind

1 1/2 teaspoons ground cinnamon

1 teaspoon vanilla extract

Frosting:
1 1/4 cups confectioners' sugar

1 tablespoon milk

2 teaspoons lemon juice

1 teaspoon vanilla extract

In large bowl of electric mixer, combine 2 1/2 cups flour, yeast, and sugar. In saucepan, combine consomme and butter. Heat to lukewarm (110°F.). Add to dry ingredients with egg. Beat at high speed for 2 minutes. Stir in remaining flour to make a stiff dough. On lightly floured board, knead until smooth (about 5 minutes). Place in greased bowl, turning once. Cover; let rise in warm place until doubled (about 1 hour). Meanwhile, combine ingredients for filling; set aside. Punch down dough. On lightly floured surface, turn out dough. Cover; let rest 10 minutes. Roll dough into rectangle (20×30″). Spread with filling to 1-inch of edges. Starting from wide end, roll up tightly jelly-roll fashion. Seal edge. On greased cookie sheet, arrange seam-side down to form a large loosely-shaped coil. Cover; let rise until doubled (about 1 hour). Bake at 350°F. for 35 to 40 minutes or until done; cool. Meanwhile, combine ingredients for frosting. Beat until smooth. Drizzle over bread.

SURPRISE CORN MUFFINS

Cream of chicken soup, egg and corn muffin mix blend into a lovely batter for muffins of superb flavor.

1 can (10 3/4 ounces) condensed cream of chicken soup

2 eggs, slightly beaten

2 packages (about 8 ounces each) corn muffin mix

In bowl, blend soup and eggs. Add muffin mix, stirring until <u>just</u> blended (batter will be slightly lumpy). Spoon batter into 18 greased muffin cups, filling about 3/4 full. Bake at 375°F. for 30 minutes or until done. Remove from pan; cool.

ZUCCHINI TEA LOAF

Not long ago zucchini had to be explained as Italian squash. Since its rise to fame, it is now used in many breads. Zucchini plus asparagus soup gives this loaf a moist texture.

2 tablespoons shortening

3/4 cup sugar

1 egg, slightly beaten

1 cup all-purpose flour

1 cup whole wheat flour

2 teaspoons baking powder

1/2 teaspoon salt

1/2 teaspoon ground allspice

1/2 teaspoon ground cinnamon

1/4 teaspoon ground nutmeg

1 can (10 3/4 ounces) condensed cream of asparagus soup

1 cup chopped walnuts

1 cup shredded zucchini squash

In bowl, combine shortening and sugar until crumbly; stir in egg. Sift together flours, baking powder, salt, and spices. Add to egg mixture alternately with soup, stirring to blend after each addition. Stir in walnuts and zucchini. Pour into greased loaf pan (9×5×3"). Bake at 350°F. for 1 hour 5 minutes or until done. Remove from pan; cool.

HERBED POTATO ROLLS

Rolls from a packaged mix take on a new dimension when cream of potato soup substitutes for half of the water. Make large or small rolls and sprinkle with poppy seed.

2 packages (14 to 18 ounces each) hot roll mix

1 can (10 3/4 ounces) condensed cream of potato soup

2 teaspoons dried chives, crushed

2 teaspoons dried parsley flakes, crushed

Poppy seed

In large bowl, sprinkle yeast from roll mix on water, using one half the total amount of water. Prepare mixes as directed on packages, substituting can of soup for remaining water; add chives and parsley. Cover; let rise in warm place until doubled (30 to 45 minutes). On floured board, knead until no longer sticky (about 1 to 2 minutes). Shape into 16 large or 32 small rolls; sprinkle with poppy seed. Place on lightly greased cookie sheet. Cover; let rise in warm place until doubled (30 to 45 minutes). Bake at 375°F. for 20 minutes or until done. Remove from cookie sheet; cool.

WHEAT GERM BREAD

Homemade bread is truly a labor of love. Look at this bread's wholesome ingredients ... whole wheat flour, wheat germ and molasses ... with a light onion flavor from soup.

4 cups whole wheat flour	1/3 cup shortening
2 cups all-purpose flour	1/3 cup light molasses
1 cup milk	2 packages active dry yeast
1 cup wheat germ	3 tablespoons sugar
1 can (10 1/2 ounces) condensed onion soup	1 teaspoon salt

Combine whole wheat and all-purpose flours; set aside. Stir milk into wheat germ; let stand until milk is absorbed. In saucepan, combine soup, shortening, and molasses. Heat, stirring until shortening is dissolved. Cool to lukewarm (110°F.). In large bowl of electric mixer, combine 3 cups flour mixture, yeast, sugar, salt, and wheat germ mixture. Beat at low speed, gradually adding soup mixture. Stir in remaining flour to make a stiff dough. On lightly floured board, knead until smooth (about 5 minutes). Place in greased bowl, turning once. Cover; let rise in warm place until doubled (about 1 hour 30 minutes). Punch down dough; divide in half. For each loaf, on lightly floured board, roll half of dough into rectangle (15×8"). Starting at narrow end, roll up jelly-roll fashion; turn under ends and seal. Place in greased glass loaf pans (8×4×3"). Cover; let rise until doubled (about 1 hour 30 minutes). Bake at 350°F. for 50 minutes or until done. Remove from pans; cool.

CHEESED PAN ROLLS

Great for breakfast or brunch with sausage and eggs.

1 package (about 14 to 18 ounces) hot roll mix	2 eggs, slightly beaten
1/4 cup warm water	1/3 cup grated Parmesan cheese
1 can (11 ounces) condensed Cheddar cheese soup	1 tablespoon dried parsley flakes
	1 package (about 8 ounces) corn muffin mix

In large bowl, sprinkle yeast from roll mix on water; stir until dissolved. Blend in soup, eggs, cheese, and parsley. Add corn muffin mix and flour mixture from roll mix; stir until well blended. Cover; let rise in warm place until doubled (30 to 45 minutes). On floured board, knead until no longer sticky (about 1 to 2 minutes). Shape into 24 round rolls. Place in 2 lightly greased 8-inch round baking pans. Cover; let rise in warm place until doubled (30 to 45 minutes). Bake at 375°F. for 20 minutes or until done. Remove from pan; cool.

QUICK CHEDDAR BREAD

Convenience is the theme here. A food processor chops the onion, cheese and biscuit mix come from packages, while canned condensed soup binds the ingredients together.

1 cup finely chopped onion
2 tablespoons butter or margarine
2 cups shredded Cheddar cheese

1 can (10 3/4 ounces) condensed cream of mushroom soup
4 cups biscuit mix
2 eggs, slightly beaten
1/4 cup chopped parsley

In saucepan, cook onion in butter until tender. Remove from heat. Add 1 cup cheese and remaining ingredients. Stir until just blended (batter will be slightly lumpy). Spread evenly in 2 greased 9-inch round layer pans. Bake at 400°F. for 25 minutes. Sprinkle remaining cheese over layers; bake 15 minutes more or until done. Remove from pan; cool.

RASPBERRY CHEESE PIE

If those handsome cheese pies in bakery windows tempt you too often, you need your own recipe. Claim this raspberry-cheese pie immediately and prepare it soon.

Crumb Crust:

2 cups fine graham cracker crumbs
6 tablespoons butter or margarine, melted

1/4 cup sugar

Raspberry Layer:

2 tablespoons cornstarch
1/4 cup orange juice

1 package (10 ounces) frozen raspberries, thawed

Cheese Layer:

1 can (11 ounces) condensed Cheddar cheese soup
1 package (3 ounces) cream cheese, softened
1/4 cup light rum

2/3 cup sugar
2 eggs, separated
2 envelopes unflavored gelatine
1/2 cup heavy cream, whipped
1/4 teaspoon cream of tartar

Crust: Combine all ingredients. Press firmly into 10″ pie plate; chill.

Raspberry Layer: In saucepan, combine raspberries, orange juice, and cornstarch. Cook, stirring until thickened. Pour into crust; chill.

Cheese Layer: In saucepan, blend soup, cream cheese, rum, 1/3 cup sugar, egg yolks, and gelatine. Cook, stirring until cream cheese is melted and gelatine is dissolved. Chill until slightly thickened (20 minutes). Fold into whipped cream. In large bowl, beat egg whites and cream of tartar until foamy. Add remaining 1/3 cup sugar, 1 tablespoon at a time, beating until stiff but still shiny. Fold gelatine mixture into egg whites. Spoon over raspberry layer; chill until firm. Garnish with whipped cream and orange slices. Makes one 10-inch pie.

PUMPKIN OATMEAL COOKIES

A nourishing cookie to fill outstretched hands. Bake a batch often for school lunches, hikes and picnics.

3 cups all-purpose flour
3 teaspoons baking powder
2 tablespoons ground pumpkin pie spice
1 teaspoon salt
1 can (10 3/4 ounces) condensed cream of potato soup

2 cups packed brown sugar
1 can (about 16 ounces) pumpkin
1 cup shortening
2 eggs
2 cups quick-cooking oats, uncooked
1 1/2 cups flaked coconut
1 1/2 cups chopped walnuts

Preheat oven to 350°F. In large bowl, sift flour, baking powder, spice, and salt. Add soup, sugar, pumpkin, shortening, and eggs. Using electric mixer, beat at medium speed for 2 minutes (300 strokes with spoon), scraping sides and bottom of bowl constantly. Stir in oats, coconut, and nuts. Drop rounded teaspoonfuls on greased cookie sheet. Bake 20 minutes or until done. Frost or sprinkle with confectioners' sugar if desired. Makes about 10 dozen cookies.

PLUM PUDDING

Brandied plum puddings make excellent holiday gifts. But wait! Keep one for yourself and guests to enjoy.

1/2 cup currants
1/2 cup raisins
1/3 cup brandy
3 cups sifted all-purpose flour
1/2 cup sugar
1 teaspoon baking powder
1 teaspoon salt
1 teaspoon ground cinnamon
1/2 teaspoon ground cloves
1/2 teaspoon ground ginger

1/2 teaspoon ground nutmeg
1/2 cup chopped walnuts
1/4 cup chopped candied citron
1/4 cup chopped mixed candied fruit
1 apple, peeled and grated
1 can (10 1/2 ounces) condensed beef broth
1 cup chopped suet
1/2 cup light molasses

Soak currants and raisins in brandy for 2 hours. In large bowl, sift dry ingredients. Add currants, raisins, nuts, citron, mixed fruit, and apple; mix to coat with flour. Stir in soup, suet, and molasses; mix until well blended. Pour into 2 well-greased 1 1/2-quart molds; cover securely with foil. Place on trivet in large pan. Add boiling water to 1/2 height of mold. Cover; steam 3 hours. Remove mold from water; uncover and loosen edges of pudding with knife. Unmold while hot. Serve warm with Hard Sauce.

STEAMED BROWNIE PUDDING

Forget calorie counting as you enjoy a portion of rich steamed chocolate pudding mounded with hard sauce.

2 cups all-purpose flour
1 cup sugar
1 teaspoon baking soda
1/2 teaspoon salt
1 can (10 3/4 ounces) condensed tomato soup
3 squares (1 ounce each) unsweetened chocolate, melted

1 egg
1/4 cup shortening
2 tablespoons water
1 teaspoon vanilla extract
1 cup chopped dates
1/2 cup chopped walnuts

In large bowl of electric mixer, combine all ingredients except dates and walnuts; mix well. Stir in dates and walnuts. Pour into well-greased 1 1/2-quart ring mold; cover securely with foil. Place on trivet in large pan. Add boiling water to one-half the height of mold. Cover; steam 1 hour 30 minutes or until done. Remove mold from water. Uncover; loosen edges of pudding with knife. Serve warm with Hard Sauce.

PEACHY BRUNCH CAKE

A perfectly marvelous peachy coffee cake to take to a brunch. Bake it in the morning; take it along in the pan. Your hostess will love you.

1 package (2 layer) yellow cake mix
1 can (11 ounces) condensed Cheddar cheese soup
1/2 cup water
2 eggs
1/2 teaspoon almond extract
2 cans (16 ounces each) sliced peaches, well-drained and chopped

1/2 cup chopped almonds
3 tablespoons butter or margarine, softened
1/2 cup all-purpose flour
1/4 cup packed brown sugar
1 teaspoon ground cinnamon

Preheat oven to 350°F. Generously grease and flour a 3-quart shallow baking pan (13×9×2″). In large bowl of electric mixer, combine cake mix, soup, water, eggs, and almond extract. Beat, following package directions. Stir in peaches and almonds. Spread batter evenly in pan. Meanwhile, to make topping, cut butter into flour, sugar, and cinnamon until crumbly. Sprinkle over batter. Bake 50 minutes or until done. Serve warm.

HOLIDAY FRUITCAKE

When you bake for the holidays you expect beautiful fruitcakes. Dates, raisins and chopped candied fruit and in just-right proportions for these two loaves.

5 cups all-purpose flour	7 eggs
2 teaspoons baking powder	1 tablespoon vanilla extract
1 teaspoon ground cinnamon	2 cups chopped pitted dates
1 teaspoon ground mace	2 cups raisins
1/2 teaspoon ground nutmeg	2 1/2 cups chopped pecans
1 can (10 3/4 ounces) condensed chicken broth	2 cups shredded coconut
2 cups packed brown sugar	1 cup assorted chopped candied fruit
1 1/2 cups butter or margarine, softened	Candied cherries, cut in half
	Pecan halves

Preheat oven to 325°F. Grease 2 loaf pans (9×5×3″). In large bowl, sift 4 cups flour, baking powder, cinnamon, mace, and nutmeg. Add broth, sugar, and butter. Beat at medium speed of electric mixer for 2 minutes, scraping sides and bottom of bowl constantly. Add eggs and vanilla; beat 2 minutes more, scraping bowl often. Toss dates and raisins with remaining flour; stir into batter. Add chopped pecans, coconut, and candied fruit. Pour into loaf pans. Bake 1 hour 45 minutes or until done. Remove from pans; cool. If desired, heat orange marmalade; spoon over cakes. Arrange cherries and pecan halves on top.

PRALINE TARTS

A delightful dessert that guests will love — mini-cheesecakes topped with pecans.

Pastry for two 2-crust pies

Filling:

1 can (11 ounces) condensed Cheddar cheese soup	1/3 cup sugar
1 package (3 ounces) cream cheese, softened	2 eggs
	1/2 teaspoon vanilla
	1/2 cup chopped pecans

Topping:

2 eggs	1/4 cup sugar
3/4 cup light corn syrup	1 teaspoon vanilla

Preheat oven to 375°F. Roll pastry to 1/8-inch thickness. Cut into 16 circles (4 inch). Line well-greased muffin cups (2 3/4×1″) with pastry. To make filling: In small bowl of electric mixer, beat soup and cheese until smooth. Blend in remaining ingredients except chopped pecans. Spoon about 2 tablespoons mixture into each pastry-lined cup. Sprinkle each with 1 teaspoon pecans. To make topping: In small bowl of electric mixer, combine ingredients for topping; mix well. Carefully spoon about 4 teaspoons over pecans in each cup. Bake 35 minutes or until done. Cool slightly. Remove from pans. Serve with whipped cream.

RAISIN PIE

Walnuts, orange and spices add substantially to the taste of raisin pie. Take a peek through the lattice crust. Doesn't it look good?

2 tablespoons cornstarch	1/3 cup chopped walnuts
3/4 cup orange juice	1/2 teaspoon ground cinnamon
1 can (10 3/4 ounces) condensed	1/2 teaspoon grated orange rind
tomato soup	1/8 teaspoon ground cloves
2 cups raisins	2 tablespoons butter or margarine
2/3 cup sugar	Pastry for 2-crust pie

Preheat oven to 425°F. Mix cornstarch and 1/4 cup juice until smooth. In saucepan, combine soup, raisins, and 1/2 cup juice; bring to boil. Cover; cook over low heat 10 minutes. Stir occasionally. Add cornstarch mixture and remaining ingredients except pastry. Cook, stirring until thickened. Pour into 9″ pastry-lined pie plate. Roll out remaining pastry; cut into 1/2-inch wide strips. Crisscross strips over filling to form lattice top. Bake 25 minutes or until done.

CARROT CAKE

You can eat this cake and have your carrots, too! Through their moisture, shredded carrots increase the cake's keeping quality.

2 cups cake flour	1 teaspoon ground nutmeg
1 1/3 cups packed brown	1 can (10 3/4 ounces) condensed
sugar	tomato soup
4 teaspoons baking powder	1/2 cup shortening
1 teaspoon baking soda	2 eggs
1 teaspoon ground allspice	1/4 cup honey
1 teaspoon ground cinnamon	1 cup shredded raw carrots

Preheat oven to 350°F. Generously grease and flour a 10″ bundt pan. In large bowl of electric mixer, combine dry ingredients. Add soup and shortening. Beat at medium speed for 2 minutes (300 strokes with spoon), scraping sides and bottom of bowl constantly. Add eggs and honey. Beat 2 minutes more, scraping bowl frequently; fold in carrots. Pour into pan; bake 1 hour or until done. Let cool in pan 15 minutes; remove. Cool. Glaze with Orange Sauce if desired.

ORANGE SAUCE

Creamy orange sauce should be spread over warm cake!

1 cup packed brown sugar	1 tablespoon light corn syrup
1/2 cup orange juice	1 teaspoon baking soda
2 tablespoons butter or	1/2 cup sour cream
margarine	

In saucepan, combine all ingredients except sour cream. Bring to boil; cook over low heat 5 minutes. Blend in sour cream. Drizzle and spread glaze over warm cake. Allow cake to absorb glaze. Repeat until all glaze has been used. Makes about 1 1/2 cups.

Marvelous Ways
with Microwave

Marvelous Ways with Microwave

Microwave cooking offers another way to be creative in the kitchen — another alternative for food preparation.

Many people now are taking advantage of this cool way of cooking. Microwave cooking performs the task in a completely different manner than conventional cooking. Microwaves cause the heat to originate in the food itself, instead of relying on the transfer of heat, which is the traditional method. Thus the cool oven!

Inside every microwave oven is a magnetron tube which converts electrical energy into electromagnetic energy, sending cool microwaves into the oven cavity. Here they are absorbed into food. Molecules begin to vibrate at a tremendous rate, creating heat within the food. Rapid cooking takes place, moving from the outside edges to the center.

Cooking in these units calls for utensils which allow for microwaves to pass through them to the food. Glass, ceramic, plastics and paper are recommended rather than metal because metal reflects microwave energy back to the magnetron tube which may cause damage to it. Timing and the power settings are the controls used in microwave cooking. Except where noted, the recipes which follow were tested on "full power" in 650 watt countertop microwave ovens.

Another important point to consider in microwave cooking is the quantity of food in the oven. More food means more time is needed. While a single potato cooks in four minutes, two potatoes may take up to twice as long. Never vary the quantities in microwave recipes without also changing the timing.

A very basic question is what can be prepared in the microwave? This chapter is devoted to recipes for microwave cooking, from beverages and snacks right through to desserts. The advantages of these recipes are two-fold: you save cooking time and energy too.

The preceding photo shows the variety of creations produced with the microwave.

The Golden Ginger Chicken uses condensed golden mushroom soup, orange juice, ginger and chopped onion for a delicious sauce that was simply mixed and poured over the cooking chicken.

Another unusual main course that can also grace a buffet is Mini-Meat Loaves. In this case, condensed tomato soup is the base for a sauce spiced with thyme and sage.

For the Appetizer Party Franks, the green pepper and onion were started first in the microwave then condensed tomato soup, seasonings and frankfurters added and cooked for just 10 minutes.

For a special treat, Date Nut Bars with walnuts and spices are ready in a short time. Here, condensed tomato soup is a refreshing flavor ingredient with the dates and other aromatic seasonings.

For Pepper Steak with Polynesian flavoring, condensed beefy mushroom soup can be used as a base and mixed with pineapple, soy sauce, onion and green pepper. Preparation and cooking time are minimum and the result is a succulent main course.

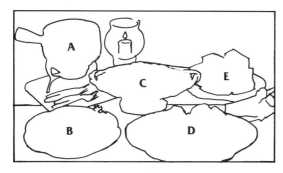

A APPETIZER PARTY FRANKS
B MINI-MEATLOAVES
    AND CARROTS AU GRATIN
C PEPPER STEAK
D GOLDEN GINGER CHICKEN
E DATE NUT BARS

APPETIZER PARTY FRANKS

Bite-size pieces of frankfurters, coated with a tomato soup mixture of peppery seasonings, go well with cold fruit punch.

1/2 cup finely chopped onion	1 tablespoon vinegar
1/3 cup finely chopped green pepper	1 tablespoon Worcestershire
2 tablespoons butter or margarine	1 teaspoon prepared mustard
	Dash hot pepper sauce
1 can (10 3/4 ounces) condensed tomato soup	1 1/2 pounds frankfurters, cut in 1-inch pieces

1. In 1 1/2-quart glass casserole, combine onion, green pepper, and butter. Cook in microwave oven 4 minutes or until vegetables are tender, stirring 1 time.

2. Add remaining ingredients. Cover with waxed paper; cook 10 minutes or until hot, stirring 3 times.

3. Let stand 5 minutes. Stir before serving. Makes about 4 cups.

SWISS FONDUE

With a microwave oven the metal fondue pot is out — the glass casserole is in! Enjoy your fondue with a green salad. For dessert? Fresh pears and apples.

1 can (11 ounces) condensed Cheddar cheese soup	1/4 teaspoon Worcestershire
8 ounces (8 slices) natural Swiss cheese, torn in pieces	1/4 teaspoon prepared mustard
	1/8 teaspoon hot pepper sauce
	French or Italian bread cubes

1. To make fondue, in 1-quart glass casserole, combine all ingredients except bread cubes.

2. Cook in microwave oven 4 to 5 minutes or until cheese melts, stirring 3 times.

3. Stir before serving. Spear bread with fork or toothpick; dip into fondue. Makes about 3 1/2 cups.

BEEF ENCHILADAS

The tortilla turns into an enchilada when it's filled with a spicy meat-soup mixture. Microwave it and use a green pepper ring garnish. Serve with a cold drink.

1 can (11 1/4 ounces) condensed chili beef soup
1/2 pound ground beef
1/4 cup ketchup
2 tablespoons chopped onion
1 teaspoon chili powder

1/2 teaspoon garlic salt
1/4 teaspoon ground cumin seed
8 corn tortillas
1/2 cup shredded Cheddar cheese
1/2 cup water

1. In 1-quart glass measuring cup, combine 1/4 cup soup, beef, ketchup, onion, and seasonings. Cook in microwave oven 5 minutes, stirring 1 time to separate meat.

2. To make enchiladas, wrap 2 tortillas in damp cloth towel; cook 30 seconds.

3. Immediately spoon about 2 tablespoons meat mixture on each tortilla; top with 1 tablespoon cheese. Tightly roll up. Place seam-side down in 1 1/2-quart shallow glass baking dish (10 × 6 × 2″). Repeat until all tortillas are filled.

4. Mix remaining soup and water; pour over enchiladas. Cover with waxed paper; cook 8 to 10 minutes or until hot, giving casserole 1/2 turn 2 times. Garnish with green pepper rings if desired. Makes 4 servings.

DUTCH CORN CHOWDER

Signs of convenience in cooking are canned condensed soups, freeze-dried chives and microwave ovens. Cook up a corn chowder in minutes. Serve with crackers.

1/2 cup chopped onion
2 tablespoons butter or margarine
1 can (10 3/4 ounces) condensed cream of potato soup
1/4 cup milk

1/4 cup water
1 can (about 16 ounces) whole kernel golden corn, undrained
1 tablespoon freeze-dried chives
Dash pepper

1. In 1 1/2-quart glass casserole, combine onion and butter. Cook in microwave oven 4 minutes or until tender, stirring 1 time.

2. Stir in remaining ingredients. Cook 8 minutes or until hot, stirring 2 times.

3. Stir before serving. Makes about 4 cups.

PEPPER STEAK

The wok gives way to the microwave. While the pepper steak cooks, prepare some rice. And do remember your chopsticks!

1 pound round steak (3/4-inch thick)
1 can (10 3/4 ounces) condensed beefy mushroom soup
1 small onion, thinly sliced
1 small green pepper, cut in strips

1 can (about 8 ounces) pineapple chunks in pure pineapple juice, undrained
1 tablespoon soy sauce
1 small tomato, cut in wedges

1. Freeze meat 1 hour to firm (makes slicing easier), slice into very thin strips.

2. In 2-quart shallow glass baking dish (12 × 8 × 2″), combine soup, onion, green pepper, pineapple, pineapple juice, and soy sauce. Cook in microwave oven 4 minutes, stirring 1 time.

3. Add meat; cook 8 minutes or until done, stirring 2 times.

4. Add tomatoes; cook 1 minute. Stir before serving. Makes about 4 cups.

SOUPERBURGER

The children's favorite souperburger becomes a "hurry" burger when it's cooked in the microwave oven. Teach them a lesson on microwaving burgers.

1 pound ground beef
1/4 cup chopped onion
1 can (10 3/4 ounces) condensed chicken gumbo soup

2 tablespoons ketchup
1 tablespoon prepared mustard
Hamburger buns, split and toasted

1. In 1 1/2-quart glass casserole, combine beef and onion. Cook in microwave oven 4 to 6 minutes, stirring 2 times; pour off fat.

2. Blend in soup, ketchup, and mustard. Cook 4 to 5 minutes or until hot, stirring 1 time. Stir before serving. Serve on buns. Makes about 3 cups.

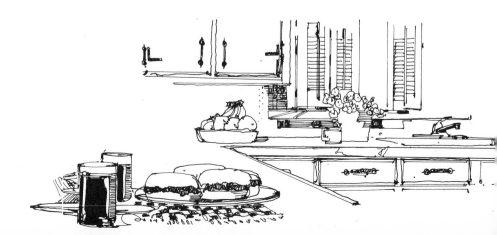

MINI-MEATLOAVES

How delightful to serve mini-meatloaves already sauced with a pleasant blend of two well liked herbs.

1 can (10 3/4 ounces) condensed tomato soup	1 teaspoon salt
2 pounds ground beef	1/4 teaspoon pepper
1/4 cup fine dry bread crumbs	1/4 teaspoon rubbed sage
1 egg, slightly beaten	1/4 teaspoon thyme leaves, crushed
1/4 cup finely chopped onion	1/4 cup water

1. Mix <u>thoroughly</u> 1/4 cup soup, beef, bread crumbs, egg, onion, salt, and 1/8 teaspoon <u>each</u> pepper, sage, and thyme. Shape <u>firmly</u> into 6 mini-meat loaves.

2. Arrange loaves spoke-fashion in 3-quart glass casserole. Cover with lid or waxed paper; cook in microwave oven 10 minutes, giving dish 1/2 turn after 5 minutes. Pour off fat.

3. Combine remaining soup, water, and seasonings; pour over loaves. Cook 5 minutes or until done, spooning sauce over loaves 1 time. Makes 6 servings.

GOLDEN GINGER CHICKEN

Frozen orange juice concentrate, ground ginger and golden mushroom soup blend into a slightly spicy mixture for chicken. The garnishes lend color.

2 pounds chicken parts	1/4 cup chopped onion
Salad oil	2 tablespoons concentrated orange juice
1 can (10 3/4 ounces) condensed golden mushroom soup	1/2 teaspoon ground ginger

1. Brush chicken with salad oil. Arrange skin-side down in 2-quart shallow glass baking dish (12 × 8 × 2"). Cover with waxed paper; cook in microwave oven 10 minutes, giving dish 1/4 turn after 5 minutes.

2. Combine soup, onion, orange juice, and ginger. Turn chicken skin-side up; pour soup mixture over chicken. Cook 10 minutes giving dish 1/4 turn after 5 minutes. Stir sauce.

3. Cook <u>uncovered</u> 4 minutes or until done. Garnish with avocado and orange slices. Makes 4 servings.

CHICKEN VERONIQUE

As a change from your usual dishes, try this classic French way of cooking chicken. Mushrooms, sauterne and, of course, white grapes spell Veronique.

2 whole chicken breasts, split (about 2 pounds)	1 medium clove garlic, minced
Salad oil	1 can (10 3/4 ounces) condensed cream of chicken soup
1 cup quartered fresh mushrooms (about 1/4 pound)	1/2 cup seedless white grapes cut in half
2 tablespoons sauterne or other dry white wine	Cooked rice

1. In 2-quart shallow glass baking dish (12 × 8 × 2″), arrange chicken skin-side down; brush with oil. Cover with waxed paper. Cook in microwave oven 8 minutes, giving dish 1/4 turn after 4 minutes.

2. Turn chicken skin-side up; add mushrooms, sauterne, and garlic. Cook 2 minutes.

3. Stir in soup; cook 10 minutes more, giving dish 1/4 turn after 5 minutes.

4. Uncover; stir sauce. Cook 3 minutes more or until done.

5. Stir in grapes; cook 1 minute.

6. Stir sauce before serving. Serve with rice. Makes 4 servings.

FILLETS OF SOLE TYROLEAN

Sole should be surrounded with the very best ingredients. That's why we chose Swiss cheese, wine, celery soup, parsley and paprika to enhance its flavor.

1/2 cup finely chopped onion	1 cup shredded Swiss cheese
2 tablespoons butter or margarine	1 tablespoon lemon juice
1 pound fillets of sole	2 teaspoons chopped parsley
1 can (10 3/4 ounces) condensed cream of celery soup	2 tablespoons Italian-flavored fine dry bread crumbs
1/4 cup chablis or other dry white wine	Paprika

1. In 2-quart shallow glass baking dish (12 × 8 × 2″), combine onion and butter. Cook in microwave oven 2 minutes or until tender, stirring one time.

2. Arrange fish in single layer in baking dish. Cook 5 minutes.

3. Meanwhile, combine soup, wine, cheese, lemon juice, and parsley. Pour over fish; top with bread crumbs and paprika.

4. Cook 8 to 10 minutes or until done, giving dish 1/4 turn one time. Makes 4 servings.

TOMATO CHEESE RABBIT

Tomato and bacon have been added to this traditional English luncheon or supper dish. Serve over toast, or spooned over toasted English muffins.

3 slices bacon
1 can (10 3/4 ounces) condensed
  cream of onion soup
1 cup shredded sharp Cheddar
  cheese
1/2 cup drained chopped
  canned tomatoes

1 teaspoon prepared mustard
1/8 teaspoon sugar
Dash pepper
Toast

1. On glass plate or in baking dish, place bacon between paper towels. Cook in microwave oven 2 1/2 to 3 minutes or until crisp; remove and crumble.

2. In 1-quart glass measuring cup, combine all ingredients except bacon and toast. Cook 5 to 7 minutes or until cheese melts, stirring 4 times.

3. Serve over toast; garnish with bacon. Makes about 2 cups.

CALICO SCRAMBLED EGGS

Nuggets of colorful mixed vegetables dot these perfectly cooked eggs . . . made moist by Cheddar cheese soup.

1/4 cup finely chopped green
  onions
2 tablespoons butter or
  margarine
1/8 teaspoon Italian
  seasoning, crushed

1 can (11 ounces) condensed
  Cheddar cheese soup
8 eggs, slightly beaten
1 cup cooked mixed vegetables
1 tablespoon grated Parmesan
  cheese
Dash pepper

1. In 1 1/2-quart shallow glass baking dish (10 × 6 × 2"), combine onion, butter, and seasoning. Cook in microwave oven 2 minutes or until tender.

2. Meanwhile, in bowl, stir soup until smooth; gradually blend in remaining ingredients. Pour into baking dish.

3. Cover with waxed paper; cook 6 to 8 minutes or until eggs are completely set, but still moist, stirring 2 times. Makes 4 servings.

ZUCCHINI MARINARA

Give an Italian accent to your meal by serving zucchini in this mildly spicy sauce.

1/4 cup finely chopped onion
1/4 cup finely chopped green
pepper
2 tablespoons butter or
margarine
1 medium clove garlic, minced
1/2 teaspoon oregano leaves,
crushed

1 medium bay leaf
1 can (10 3/4 ounces) condensed
tomato soup
1 1/2 pounds zucchini squash,
thinly sliced (about 6 cups)
1 can (about 2 ounces) sliced
mushrooms, drained

1. In 2-quart glass casserole, combine onion, green pepper, butter, and seasonings. Cook in microwave oven 4 minutes or until tender, stirring 1 time.

2. Add remaining ingredients; cover with lid or waxed paper. Cook 15 minutes or until done, stirring 3 times. Remove bay leaf. Let stand covered 5 minutes before serving. Makes about 3 1/2 cups.

CARROTS AU GRATIN

Carrots cook in a sharp cheese sauce that's creamy in consistency. Never a lump here — soup makes it smooth.

1/2 cup chopped onion
2 tablespoons butter or
margarine
1/2 teaspoon dry mustard
1/8 teaspoon pepper
1 can (10 3/4 ounces) condensed
cream of celery soup

3/4 cup milk
1 cup shredded sharp Cheddar
cheese
1 1/2 pounds carrots, cooked and
cut in strips

1. In 1 1/2-quart glass casserole, combine onion, butter, and seasonings. Cook in microwave oven 2 minutes or until tender.

2. Add remaining ingredients. Cover with lid or waxed paper. Cook 9 minutes, stirring 3 times. Stir before serving. Makes about 4 cups.

VEGETABLES ALMONDINE

Four different colored vegetables cook in cream of chicken soup along with a favorite Chinese sauce...soy. Some like extra; serve it from a cruet.

3 cups diagonally sliced celery	1 cup sliced water chestnuts
1 can (10 3/4 ounces) condensed cream of chicken soup	1 can (about 4 ounces) sliced mushrooms, drained
1/2 cup water	3 tablespoons soy sauce
1 can (12 ounces) whole kernel golden corn with sweet peppers, drained	1/4 cup toasted slivered almonds

1. In 2-quart glass casserole, cook celery in microwave oven 6 minutes or until tender, stirring 3 times.

2. Stir in remaining ingredients except almonds. Cover with lid or waxed paper. Cook 10 minutes or until hot, stirring 3 times.

3. Stir in almonds. Serve with additional soy. Makes about 4 cups.

DATE NUT BARS

This nutritious snack with fruit, nuts, oats and eggs will be popular with your family. Keep your cookie box or jar full — if you can!

1 1/2 cups cut-up pitted dates	2 teaspoons ground cinnamon
3/4 cup water	1 teaspoon ground allspice
1/4 cup sugar	1 can (10 3/4 ounces) condensed tomato soup
2 tablespoons lemon juice	1 1/3 cups packed brown sugar
1/2 cup chopped walnuts	2 eggs
1 1/2 cups all-purpose flour	1/2 cup salad oil
1 teaspoon baking powder	1 cup quick oats, uncooked
1/2 teaspoon baking soda	

1. In 2-quart glass casserole, combine dates, water, sugar, and lemon juice; cover with lid or waxed paper. Cook in microwave oven 6 minutes, stirring 2 times. Stir until mixture thickens. Add nuts; cool slightly.

2. In large bowl of electric mixer, sift flour, baking powder, baking soda, and spices. Add soup, brown sugar, eggs, and oil. Beat at medium speed for 2 minutes; stir in oats.

3. Spread half of soup mixture in greased 2-quart shallow baking dish (12 × 8 × 2″). Spoon date filling on soup mixture; top with remaining soup mixture.

4. Place baking dish on inverted 1-quart casserole in microwave oven; cook 15 minutes or until done, giving dish 1/4 turn every 4 minutes.

5. Place baking dish directly on heatproof surface. Let cool completely before cutting.

TOMATO BEEF TODDY

Mix this drink ahead except for the vodka. Just as your guests arrive, pop it into the microwave. Offer them piping hot toddy with light green celery sticks.

1 can (10 1/2 ounces) condensed beef broth
2 cups "V-8" juice
1 teaspoon lemon juice

1/8 teaspoon basil leaves, crushed
4 to 6 ounces vodka
Celery sticks

1. In 1-quart glass measuring cup, combine all ingredients except vodka and celery sticks. Cook in microwave oven 8 minutes or until hot.

2. Stir in vodka. Serve in mugs with celery stick stirrers. Makes about 3 1/2 cups.

CHALET CHICKEN

Four convenience foods are an integral part of this casserole. Chunk white chicken, condensed soup, frozen peas and quick-cooking rice contribute to easy meals.

1 can (10 3/4 ounces) condensed cream of mushroom soup
3/4 cup water
1/4 cup chablis or other dry white wine
2 teaspoons soy sauce

2 cans (5 ounces each) chunk white chicken
1 package (10 ounces) frozen peas, cooked and drained
1 cup quick-cooking rice, uncooked
2 tablespoons chopped pimiento

1. In 1 1/2-quart glass casserole, combine soup, water, wine, and soy sauce. Stir in remaining ingredients.

2. Cover with lid or waxed paper; cook in microwave oven 15 minutes or until done, stirring 3 times.

3. Let stand covered 5 minutes. Stir before serving. Makes about 5 cups.

CHEESECAKE PIE

You've never had a faster baking cheesecake. This combination cheesecake-pie has a delicious light lemon topping highlighted with a little vanilla.

Crumb Crust:

6 tablespoons butter or margarine

2 cups fine graham cracker or vanilla wafer crumbs

1/4 cup sugar

Filling:

12 ounces cream cheese, softened

2/3 cup sugar

3 eggs

1 can (11 ounces) condensed Cheddar cheese soup

2 tablespoons lemon juice

1 teaspoon grated lemon rind

1 teaspoon vanilla extract

1/4 teaspoon almond extract

Topping:

1 cup sour cream

1/4 cup sugar

1 teaspoon grated lemon rind

1 teaspoon vanilla extract

To make crust:

1. In 1-cup glass measuring cup, heat butter in microwave oven 1 minute or until melted.
2. Combine with crumbs and sugar. Press firmly into 10-inch glass pie plate. Chill 1 hour.

To make filling:

1. With electric mixer, beat cream cheese until smooth. Add sugar and eggs alternately. Blend in <u>1 cup</u> soup, lemon juice, rind, and extracts. Pour into chilled pie crust.
2. Cook on medium setting for 25 minutes, giving plate 1/4 turn every 5 minutes.

To make topping:

1. Blend sour cream, remaining 1/4 cup soup, sugar, lemon rind, and vanilla. Spread on pie; cool.
2. Chill. Top with prepared fruit pie filling.

Campbell Classics

Campbell Classics

Campbell Classics

Probably the greatest testimonial to a recipe is its ability to stand the test of time. Have you ever wondered how some of the most popular ones in use today were developed, or from where they originated?

Many classics in the food world have a long history and have traveled great distances. In Europe and other parts of the world, traditional ways of preparing foods, although many times not written down in a formal way, have been handed down through families from generation to generation for hundreds of years. The history of America's culinary classics may not be as old but it is as interesting.

For instance the use of Campbell's condensed soups as cooking ingredients started a few years after World War I. A number of ways in which they were used in recipes have become classics over the years and have been selected for this chapter.

Most likely there will be one or two that seem to be familiar. Perhaps you had been introduced to them in your grandmother's kitchen. It's possible that a friend passed the recipes on to her or she might have found the idea or serving suggestion in an early Campbell Soup publication.

The first booklet published by Campbell Soup Company in 1905 was titled "Just As Easy." At a time when all soups had to be started from scratch and simmered for hours, it stressed the ease and convenience of using canned condensed soup. One of the most charming aspects of the booklet was the cheerful Campbell Kids illustrations and verses like:

"If I were you and you were me
we would eat the same thing, don't you see,
and here's what the same thing would be:
Campbell's soups"

In 1910 the "Menu Cookbook" was printed which outlined menu suggestions for breakfast, lunch and dinner for an entire month. A short preface to the booklet set the tone, "Upon the selection of the soup depends, to no inconsiderable degree, the success of the dinner."

"Help for the Hostess", published in 1916, was the first booklet to use soup as an ingredient. It was written around successful hostessing, either with a maid or without! Although that aspect no longer applies to most households, one point toward the end of the book still holds true, "One of the most important and economical uses of Campbell's soup is for sauces and stock."

A glance at the preceding photo showing five Campbell Classics reinforces this point. Golden and succulent Glorified Chicken uses condensed Cheddar cheese soup for a delicious and dependable sauce. For variety, condensed cream of celery, chicken or mushroom soups could be substituted. It can be cooked in either a skillet or in the oven and served with a flair as if one were sharing a special family heirloom.

Best Ever Meat Loaf can be done with a number of variations but the basic moistening ingredients which bind the mixture together and flavor it are one egg and a can of condensed cream of mushroom or golden mushroom soup. With the addition of nutmeg, sour cream and thinly sliced cucumber garnishes, it can become a Swedish Meat Loaf; with mashed potatoes and shredded Cheddar cheese, a Frosted Meat Loaf; or with frozen patty shells or refrigerator crescent dinner rolls, a variation of Beef Wellington. Adaptability is certainly a major characteristic of this recipe and accounts for its perennial popularity.

Versatile condensed cream of mushroom soup blended with just a little soy sauce and milk is a highlight of Green Bean Bake, a crunchy and delicious vegetable casserole. This recipe is so dependable that it is not unusual to find one or even two Green Bean Bakes at a church or community supper.

Two recipes illustrated in the photo feature condensed tomato soup, one of the oldest and most popular of the Campbell's condensed soups. They are the Tomato Spice Cake and Tomato French Dressing. The Dressing using vinegar, salad oil and a little dry mustard can be made in a blender or as in the days before highly mechanized kitchens, shaken in a covered jar. It, too, lends itself to variation with the addition of crumbled bacon or blue cheese.

The Tomato Spice Cake is a precursor to the many fine recipes in the Fresh Baked Breads and Delectable Desserts chapter, but the principle that it uses is the same: condensed soup with eggs and perhaps other liquids are excellent ingredients for the batter. This recipe can take the form of a frosted layer cake, a rectangular loaf or a round Bundt cake sprinkled with sugar.

For more than three generations, these recipes and others in this section have been enjoyed and, in a nostalgic sense, treasured. In this chapter you may discover some pleasant remembrances from your own past and find other recipes that will become your own classics.

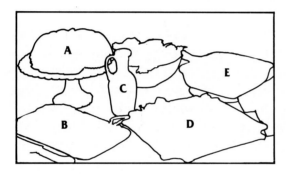

A TOMATO SPICE CAKE
B BEST EVER MEAT LOAF
C TOMATO FRENCH DRESSING
D GLORIFIED CHICKEN
E GREEN BEAN BAKE

PUREE MONGOLE

Condensed green pea and tomato soups unite with curry powder to make a quick version of this popular soup.

1 can (11 1/4 ounces) condensed green pea soup	**1 cup milk**
1 can (10 3/4 ounces) condensed tomato soup	**1 cup water** **Dash curry powder**

In saucepan, blend soups, milk, water, and curry powder. Heat; stir occasionally. Makes about 4 1/2 cups.

BEST EVER MEAT LOAF

This meat loaf is entitled to the award "best ever". With its many variations it's suitable for both family and company fare.

1 can (10 3/4 ounces) condensed cream of mushroom or golden mushroom soup **2 pounds ground beef** **1/2 cup fine dry bread crumbs**	**1 egg, slightly beaten** **1/3 cup finely chopped onion** **1 teaspoon salt** **1/3 cup water**

Mix thoroughly 1/2 cup soup, beef, bread crumbs, egg, onion, and salt. Shape firmly into loaf (8 × 4″); place in shallow baking pan. Bake at 375°F. for 1 hour 15 minutes. In saucepan, blend remaining soup, water, and 2 to 3 tablespoons drippings. Heat; stir occasionally. Serve with loaf. Makes 6 to 8 servings.

Frosted Meat Loaf: Prepare loaf as above; bake for 1 hour. Frost loaf with 4 cups mashed potatoes; sprinkle with shredded Cheddar cheese. Bake 15 minutes more.

Swedish Meat Loaf: Add 1/2 teaspoon nutmeg to loaf. Blend remaining soup with 1/3 cup sour cream; omit drippings and water. Serve over loaf; sprinkle with additional nutmeg. Garnish with thinly sliced cucumber.

Meat Loaf Wellington:
Crescent Rolls (Refrigerated): Prepare loaf as above. Bake at 375°F. for 1 hour. Spoon off fat. Separate 1 package (8 ounces) refrigerated crescent dinner rolls; place crosswise over top and down sides of meat loaf, overlapping slightly. Bake 15 minutes more.

Patty Shells: Thaw 1 package (10 ounces) frozen patty shells. Prepare loaf as above. Bake at 375°F. for 30 minutes. Spoon off fat. Increase oven temperature to 400°F. On floured board, roll 5 patty shells into rectangle (12×8″); prick several times with fork. Cover top and sides of loaf with pastry. Decorate top with remaining patty shell, rolled and cut into fancy shapes. Bake 45 minutes more or until golden brown. Serve with sauce.

EASY POT ROAST

There's no onion chopping here — not even with a food processor. Convenient onion soup takes care of the onion flavor and the liquid in cooking this roast.

3 to 4-pound boneless beef pot roast
1 can (10 1/2 ounces) condensed
    onion, golden mushroom, or
    cream of mushroom soup

In large heavy pan, brown meat on all sides (use shortening if necessary); pour off fat. Stir in soup. Cover; cook over low heat 2 1/2 to 3 hours. Stir occasionally. Remove meat. To thicken, gradually blend 1/4 cup water into 2 to 4 tablespoons flour until smooth; slowly stir into soup. Cook, stirring until thickened. Serve with meat. Makes 6 to 8 servings.

SALISBURY STEAK

This "steak" recipe gets its name from the late Dr. Salisbury who put some patients on a ground beef diet. Everyone loves this version — even non-dieters.

1 can (10 3/4 ounces) condensed   **1/4 cup finely chopped onion**
    golden mushroom soup   **1 egg, slightly beaten**
1 1/2 pounds ground beef   **1/3 cup water**
1/2 cup fine dry bread crumbs

Mix <u>thoroughly</u> 1/4 cup soup, beef, bread crumbs, onion, and egg; shape <u>firmly</u> into 6 patties. In skillet, brown patties (use shortening if necessary); pour off fat. Blend in remaining soup and water. Cover; cook over low heat 20 minutes or until done. Stir occasionally. Makes 6 servings.

PERFECT TUNA CASSEROLE

How many ovens in the United States or around the world have baked this famous casserole? Don't venture a guess because many are baking right now!

1 can (10 3/4 ounces) condensed   **2 hard-cooked eggs, sliced**
    cream of celery or   **1 cup cooked peas**
    mushroom soup   **1/2 cup slightly crumbled**
1/4 cup milk   **potato chips**
1 can (about 7 ounces) tuna,
    drained and flaked

In 1-quart casserole, blend soup and milk; stir in tuna, eggs, and peas. Bake at 350°F. for 25 minutes or until hot; stir. Top with chips; bake 5 minutes more. Makes about 4 cups.

BEEF STROGANOFF

Beef, sour cream, paprika, mushrooms and noodles add up to give this recipe its name. Thousands of diners have enjoyed this quick version using mushroom soup.

1 pound boneless round
  steak (3/4-inch thick)
1/2 cup chopped onion
2 tablespoons butter or
  margarine
1 can (10 3/4 ounces) condensed
  golden mushroom or
  cream of mushroom soup

1/2 cup sour cream
1/4 cup water
1/2 teaspoon paprika
Cooked noodles

Freeze meat 1 hour to firm (makes slicing easier); slice into <u>very</u> thin strips. In skillet, cook onion in butter until <u>just</u> tender; push to one side. Add meat; cook until color <u>just</u> changes. Add remaining ingredients except noodles. Heat; stir occasionally. Serve over noodles. Makes about 3 1/2 cups.

OLD FASHIONED CHICKEN AND NOODLES

A traditional recipe in the best sense of the word because it has been handed down from generation to generation.

1 can (10 3/4 ounces) condensed
  cream of chicken soup
1/3 cup milk
1/4 teaspoon dry mustard
1/4 teaspoon salt
Generous dash pepper
1 1/2 cups diced cooked chicken

2 cups cooked noodles
1 can (about 8 ounces) whole
  kernel golden corn, drained
1/4 cup finely chopped onion
1/4 cup buttered bread crumbs
1 hard-cooked egg, sliced

In 1 1/2-quart casserole, blend soup, milk, mustard, salt, and pepper. Stir in chicken, noodles, corn, and onion. Bake at 400°F. for 25 minutes or until hot; stir. Top with bread crumbs. Bake 5 minutes more. Garnish with egg. Makes about 4 1/2 cups.

BAKED MACARONI 'N' CHEESE

Macaroni mingles with sauce made from cream of mushroom soup and Cheddar cheese. Topped with fried onions, it's a casserole that will be empty in minutes.

1 can (10 3/4 ounces) condensed cream of mushroom soup	Generous dash pepper
1/2 cup milk	3 cups cooked elbow macaroni
1/2 teaspoon prepared mustard	2 cups shredded Cheddar cheese
	1 cup French fried onions

In 1 1/2-quart casserole, blend soup, milk, mustard, and pepper. Stir in macaroni and 1 1/2 cups cheese. Bake at 400°F. for 25 minutes or until hot; stir. Top with onions and remaining cheese; bake 5 minutes more or until cheese melts. Makes about 4 1/2 cups.

PARMESAN NOODLES

As a main course at lunch or a side dish at dinner, creamy mushroom soup and cheese blend to coat the perfectly cooked pasta.

1 can (10 3/4 ounces) condensed cream of mushroom soup	3 cups hot cooked noodles
3/4 cup milk	1/4 cup butter or margarine
1/2 cup grated Parmesan cheese	

In large saucepan, stir soup until smooth; blend in milk and cheese. Heat; stir occasionally. Just before serving, toss hot noodles with butter; combine with soup mixture. Serve with additional cheese. Makes about 3 1/2 cups.

EASY SOUFFLE

A perfect souffle is the envy of every good cook. This one is easy and delicious.

1 can (10 3/4 ounces) condensed cream of celery soup	1 cup shredded sharp process cheese
	6 eggs, separated

In saucepan, combine soup and cheese. Heat slowly until cheese melts. Stir occasionally. Remove from heat. Beat egg yolks until thick and lemon-colored; gradually stir in soup mixture. In large bowl, using clean beater, beat egg whites until stiff peaks form; fold in soup mixture. Pour into ungreased 2-quart casserole. Bake at 300°F. for 1 to 1 hour 15 minutes or until souffle is brown. Serve immediately. Makes 4 to 6 servings.

PILAF

Noodle and rice fans have raved over this recipe for years. Small wonder when condensed chicken broth flavors both foods.

1/2 cup fine noodles, broken in pieces	1 can (10 3/4 ounces) condensed chicken broth
2 tablespoons butter or margarine	1/3 cup water
	1/2 cup raw regular rice

In saucepan, brown noodles in butter; stir often. Add remaining ingredients. Bring to a boil; reduce heat. Cover; cook over low heat 20 minutes or until liquid is absorbed. Stir occasionally. Makes about 2 cups.

GREEN BEAN BAKE

Back to the ever popular Green Bean Bake recipe. This is an all-time favorite with adults and children alike.

1 can (10 3/4 ounces) condensed cream of mushroom soup	2 packages (9 ounces each) frozen green beans, cooked and drained
1/2 cup milk	1 can (3 1/2 ounces) French fried onions
1 teaspoon soy sauce	
Dash pepper	

In 1 1/2-quart casserole, stir soup, milk, soy, and pepper until smooth; mix in green beans and 1/2 can onions. Bake at 350°F. for 25 minutes; stir. Top with remaining onions. Bake 5 minutes more. Makes about 4 cups.

SCALLOPED POTATOES

Disappointment of curdled scalloped potatoes vanished when this recipe appeared on the scene.

1 can (10 3/4 ounces) condensed cream of celery or mushroom soup	Dash pepper
	4 cups thinly sliced potatoes
1/3 to 1/2 cup milk	1 small onion, thinly sliced
1/4 cup chopped parsley	1 tablespoon butter or margarine
	Dash paprika

Combine soup, milk, parsley, and pepper. In 1 1/2-quart casserole, arrange alternate layers of potatoes, onion, and sauce. Dot top with butter; sprinkle with paprika. Cover; bake at 375°F. for 1 hour. Uncover; bake 15 minutes more or until potatoes are done. Makes about 3 1/2 cups.

TOMATO FRENCH DRESSING

Poured from a cruet or spooned from a silver dish, this smooth dressing coats endless types of salads. Variations are limitless with today's new products.

1 can (10 3/4 ounces) condensed
   tomato soup
1/2 cup salad oil

1/4 cup vinegar
1/2 teaspoon dry mustard

In covered jar or shaker, combine ingredients; shake well before using. (Or mix in an electric blender.) Makes about 1 1/2 cups.
<u>Variations:</u> To 1 recipe of Tomato French Dressing add any one of the following:
- 4 slices bacon, cooked and crumbled
- 1/4 cup crumbled blue cheese
- 1 medium clove garlic, minced
- 1/4 cup sweet pickle relish

DRESSING LAMAZE

When sauce chefs have time, their active minds and hands work miracles. A creative chef developed this cold dressing for shrimp, and shared his recipe.

1 can (10 3/4 ounces) condensed
   tomato soup
1 cup mayonnaise
1/4 cup India or sweet pickle relish

1 hard-cooked egg, chopped
1/2 teaspoon grated onion
1/2 teaspoon prepared mustard
1 tablespoon lemon juice

Blend soup and mayonnaise. Add remaining ingredients; mix well. Chill. Serve with cooked shrimp or salad greens. Makes about 2 1/2 cups.

ALL 'ROUND TOMATO BARBECUE SAUCE

Through several decades, thousands of broiler-fryers, pound after pound of franks and hamburgers, and many steaks have been brushed with this tomato soup sauce.

1 can (10 3/4 ounces) condensed
   tomato soup
2 to 4 tablespoons sweet
   pickle relish

1/4 cup finely chopped onion
1 tablespoon brown sugar
1 tablespoon vinegar
1 tablespoon Worcestershire

In saucepan, combine ingredients. Cover; cook over low heat 10 minutes. Stir occasionally. Makes about 1 1/2 cups.

TOMATO SPICE CAKE

The popularity of this old time favorite spans many years. Tomato soup adds the unique flavor found in this cake.

2 1/4 cups cake flour or 2 cups
    all-purpose flour
1 1/3 cups sugar
4 teaspoons baking powder
1 teaspoon baking soda
1 1/2 teaspoons allspice
1 teaspoon cinnamon

1/2 teaspoon ground cloves
1 can (10 3/4 ounces) condensed
    tomato soup
1/2 cup shortening
2 eggs
1/4 cup water

Preheat oven to 350°F. Generously grease and flour 2 round layer pans, 8 or 9″, or an oblong pan, 13×9×2″. Measure dry ingredients into large bowl. Add soup and shortening. Beat at low to medium speed for 2 minutes (300 strokes with a spoon), scraping sides and bottom of bowl constantly. Add eggs and water. Beat 2 minutes more, scraping bowl frequently. Pour into pans. Bake 35 to 40 minutes. Let stand in pans 10 minutes; remove. Cool. Frost with Cream Cheese Frosting.

Bundt Pan: Proceed as above. Bake in well-greased and lightly floured 2 1/2-quart bundt pan at 350°F. for 50 to 60 minutes or until done. Cool right-side-up in pan 15 minutes; remove from pan. Cool. If desired, sprinkle with confectioners' sugar.

GLORIFIED CHICKEN

A recipe with a few ingredients might be thought of as dull. Not so, when the chicken can be cooked or baked in a choice of delicious condensed soups.

2 pounds chicken parts
2 tablespoons shortening

1 can (10 3/4 ounces) condensed
    Cheddar cheese, cream of celery,
    chicken, or mushroom soup

In skillet, brown chicken in shortening; pour off fat. Stir in soup. Cover; cook over low heat 45 minutes or until tender. Stir occasionally. Makes 4 servings.

Oven Method: In shallow baking dish (12×8×2″), arrange chicken skin-side down. Pour 2 tablespoons melted butter over chicken. Bake at 400°F. for 20 minutes. Turn chicken; bake 20 minutes more. Stir soup; pour over chicken. Bake 20 minutes more or until done. Stir sauce before serving.

What is Metric?

Someday the metric system of measurement will embrace the entire world. Already, every industrialized country except the United States is using it, and the U.S. is certainly well on its way, as anyone who has recently shopped for food can confirm. More and more of the food consumers purchase is in grams and kilograms of weight instead of ounces and pounds. Or in liters in place of pints, quarts and gallons. Careful consumers simply cannot afford to ignore this important and far-reaching development.

KITCHEN METRICS

Metric packaging and metric recipes make metric measuring utensils a must. Here are the basics:

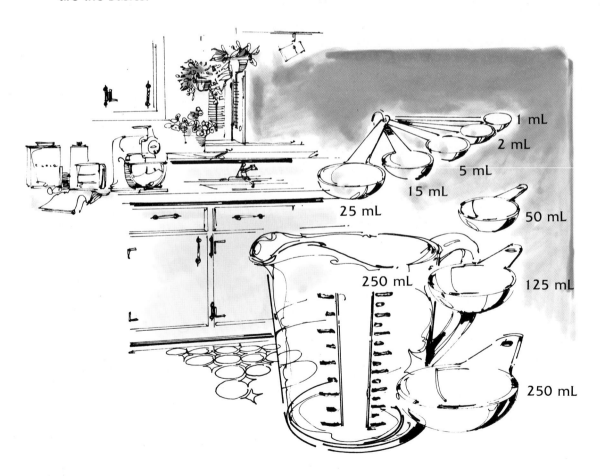

Think of all the thermometers you use in the kitchen — meat, candy, oven, freezer and room thermometers. Each will eventually be calibrated in degrees Celsius. For example:

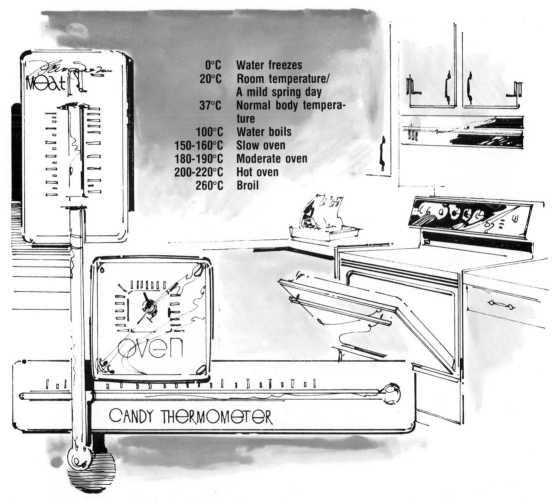

0°C	Water freezes
20°C	Room temperature/ A mild spring day
37°C	Normal body temperature
100°C	Water boils
150-160°C	Slow oven
180-190°C	Moderate oven
200-220°C	Hot oven
260°C	Broil

Increasingly, new recipes are being published which reflect these changes. Don't be reluctant to begin adding them to your collection of old favorites.

Index

C

D

E